PILLARS Of Success

INSIGH
SEVIERVILLE, TE

D1213406

Disclaimer: This book is a compilation of ideas from numerous experts who have each contributed a chapter. As such, the views expressed in each chapter are of those who were interviewed and not necessarily of the interviewer or Insight Publishing.

Published by Insight Publishing Company
P.O. Box 4189
Sevierville, Tennessee 37864

10 9 8 7 6 5 4 3 2

Printed in The United States of America

ISBN: 1-60013-027-5

Table Of Contents

A Message From The Publisher

It seems as though it was only yesterday when we were in the planning stages of this book. We wanted to find an outstanding group of professionals who have important insights to share about success and how they achieved it. Within the pages of this book you will discover that we were able to find several men and women of distinction who can give you an insider's grasp of what it takes to reach your full potential and to achieve the success you want in life.

If you spend time with a child you will soon notice how vital the questions why and how are to learning. If you've not asked how or why lately, chances are you've neglected to stretch the boundaries of what you know. Maybe you've become so bogged down in the day-to-day routines of life that you have lost the natural curiosity necessary for growth. *Pillars of Success* was put together as a comprehensive resource to help you expand your horizons and answer those important how and why questions.

In some of the interviews I asked what obstacles our authors experienced on their way to success. I think some of the answers may surprise you. Our "pillars of success" are candid and their anecdotes will amuse and enlighten you. Their experiences will open up new channels of information that you can use to enrich your life.

It is my privilege to invite you to take some time out for yourself and become inspired all over again to reach higher and turn your dreams into reality.

Interviews conducted by:
David E. Wright
President, International Speakers Network

Chapter One

JEFF GEE

David E. Wright (Wright)

Jeff Gee is CEO of MJ Learning a $10 million dollar management training company founded in 1982 with offices in the USA, Australia and the UK. Recognized worldwide as an outstanding speaker, motivator, instructor and consultant Jeff challenges his audiences to go for it 100 percent and when they do, everything changes in both their personal and professional life.

Author of three books published by McGraw-Hill: *The Winner's Attitude, Super Service,* and *The Customer Service Manager's Toolkit,* Jeff has spent over thirty-five years helping corporations reach and sustain excellence.

Featured on major television and radio networks, Jeff has shared his expertise and knowledge on customer loyalty to millions. Consultant to fortune 500 companies worldwide Jeff gets people to take responsibility and be their personal best every day.

Brought to the U.S. from the U.K by a multinational company to improve sales and employee productivity Jeff increased U.S. sales by 60 percent in just two years. During the process, he realized there was a real need to provide amazing customer service and excellence to corporate America; that was the beginning of MJ Learning.

Training over 60,000 people each year Jeff's company has an extensive client list which includes: Abbot Laboratories, Baxter, BP Amoco, Computer Associates, CDW, DeVry University, Follett Publishing, GE financing, GE Healthcare, Lucas Aerospace, MB Financial, Motorola, National Education Corp., Nike, Nutrasweet, Pepsi, Siemens, Advocate Healthcare, Tap Pharmaceuticals, Time Warner, TTX, and United Airlines.

Jeff Gee, welcome to *Pillars of Success!*

Jeff Gee (Gee)

Thank you David. It's a pleasure; I'm looking forward to this.

Wright

So many companies and speakers focus on customer service, so what makes your approach so unique?

Gee

I think the biggest thing we look at, David, is in fact two points. One is that we talk to people about customer service as an individual thing. We talk to them about the fact that it's got nothing to do with the company you work for, it's actually got nothing to do with the customer—whether they're good, bad or ugly. It has to do with you—how you're actually leading your life, how great you are at work (i.e., are you being amazing or are you just doing your job). We want them to take ownership and take responsibility for the interaction they're going to have with other human beings so that they don't have to be at the mercy of the customer, the company, management decisions, the weather or traffic—they can actually control their own existence.

The other thing we talk to them about is how to fortify this customer service program so that it becomes a way of life for them—it's not just an event—so they actually practice it every day. We have things for them to do on a daily basis, during a minimum twelve-month process so that we can actually start to see behavior changes taking place.

These are the two major things I think make us very different from the usual customer service program.

Wright

In your book, *Super Service*, the subtitle is: *Even when you don't feel like it! Even when they don't deserve it!* Can you explain how you do that?

Gee

Absolutely. All of us go through problems in life where a particular day just isn't working. We get into the office and maybe we've experienced some road rage on the way, we've got forty-eight e-mails waiting for us, and we're really having a bad day. Then there's an angry customer on the phone and it all starts to be too much. I think that's called "life"—life just doing its thing. Water's wet, rocks are hard, and life keeps doing its thing.

We want to look at what choices can be made during a negative day or event that's making you feel bad. You have a choice to make about how you want to be in this particular situation; that's basically all we have as human beings. You can't change the weather, you can't change the company's decision(s) or their policies, and you can't change a customer who's coming in very angry. What you can do though is make choices about how you're going to react to those things that are unpleasant. Do you want to be great or do you want to succumb to the unhappiness and have a miserable day, infect everybody around you and perhaps upset more customers? That's what we mean about super service, even when you don't feel like it and even when they don't deserve it. You can still be amazing because you can make a choice about which way you want to handle that particular event.

Wright

So how do you make that choice every day?

Gee

This is the sixty-four-thousand-dollar question. According to the "triune brain theory" developed by Dr. Paul MacLean, Chief of Brain Evolution and Behavior at the National Institutes of Health, we have an amazing brain, which is actually divided into three separate sections. We have—for want of a better term—what MacLean terms a "reptilian" brain which is located in the base of the skull, emerging from the spinal column. It looks after our system. In fact, most of us have no idea what's going on in our body at all. For example, we're not consciously aware all the time that we're breathing—we don't think about it—it just happens. Our heart is pumping blood around us, and we're not conscious of it because the reptilian brain handles all of that for us—it frees us up to be amazing. The reptilian brain is quite extraordinary because it really does handle everything.

I ask a lot of my people: how long would you live if you were in charge of your heart beating? The answer is: not very long because it would be too much work. The reptilian brain handles everything and it's pumping blood through your heart every year—four Olympic size swimming pools full of blood. It's amazing!

We've got these blood cells, we've so many of them it's ridiculous— we can't count them, there are billions and billions. Each blood cell has nearly three million molecules inside it. Inside each of those three million molecules—in each one—is an atom oscillating up to 10,000 times per second. It's just quite staggering what's automatically going on inside us.

Of course, when an atom is oscillating at 10,000 times per second it's actually producing energy. The amazing thing is that, as human beings, we have a huge amount of energy inside of us. The problem is, as we get older, we actually just want to take it easy when the reality is we've got enough energy to do whatever we want to do. There are people running marathons; there are people on the Olympic team; there are people climbing Everest with no different body than yours except they chose to do it and they have unlimited energy, just as we have, except we've forgotten it because we want to take it easy.

If you look at children you can see the kind of energy they can put out. We've got this wonderful reptilian brain that looks after our body and allows us to have unlimited energy and the ability to do anything we want so we can be amazing.

The reptilian brain is into survival—that's basically what an animal does—it survives. There's a term "fight or flight;" those are the choices animals have when threatened—the animal can either run away if something bigger comes toward it or it can fight something that's smaller—it just wants to survive the day. I will jokingly ask, "Have you ever seen a giraffe with a five-year plan?" There's nothing going on, it only wants to get through the day—the giraffe is in survival mode only.

When you're in survival mode you're operating in fear and everything's a problem. That's why animals spend most of their day sleeping, then eating, and reproducing. There's really not a lot going on, they just want to get through the day.

Our brain is there to help us survive the day and to make sure nothing nasty happens. I ask my people, "Have you ever seen a dog volunteer?" Well of course not! They wouldn't dream of volunteering because then the dog would be in the spotlight. Something could happen to it—it could get killed and eaten. Animals don't volunteer, they don't push, they just watch all the time. If they can sleep, they're very happy. So that's the animal brain that we have in us.

Then there is what is called the "mammalian brain." The mammalian brain is also referred to as the "limbic brain" because it extends around and off the reptilian brain in a dog-leg shape that resembles a limb. It handles complex emotions such as love, indignation, compassion, envy, and hope. Like the reptile brain, the mammalian brain can be stimulated indirectly by words. It expresses itself exclusively in the form of feelings.

Then we've got the neocortex, which is something we share with the higher apes, although ours is a bit more sophisticated. Our neocortex is where we process abstract thought, words and symbols, logic and time. As a human being, using the neocortex—my human brain—I can achieve anything I put my mind to. How do we know that? We just look around at the world with the amazing things we've managed to build and construct such as computers—they were actually invented by a human brain—so if you think a computer is amazing, the human brain is far beyond that.

We can do anything that we put our minds to. We can send a probe to Mars, it's so far away we've no concept of the distance, but we sent one. It landed and it picked up things and brought them back to us. We're amazing, amazing human beings! We can literally do anything.

Now, there's a little thing happening inside us called a "reticular activating system." It goes between the human and the animal brain. It's literally like a toggle switch and it's operating between the human and the animal brain all day long, depending on our emotional state. That's where we get problems.

I talk to people about the voices that are inside their heads or, to make it more acceptable, we'll call them thoughts. How many thoughts do you have a day? Well, billions of them. I call them voices—the little voice that talks to you inside your head. We've usually got two of them—one's the human voice and one's the animal voice. The animal voice is only into survival, so it's the one that gets angry, upset, depressed, envious, and jealous because it really doesn't want to do anything, but it wants everything. It just wants to sleep and take it easy. It tells you that you deserve a rest—you've been working like a dog. (We very rarely see dogs work so I'm not sure where that saying came from.)

We live in a society where we are controlled and governed by fear, and fear is an animal instinct to survive. When we come from fear, we're not in our human brain, so we end up doing all of those things we don't really want to do such as get angry, experience road rage, get upset with people, get intimidated, worried, depressed, etc. When we're in the human brain we literally transcend—we end the trance of being in the animal brain, and we can then connect with everybody we meet. We're the only beings on the planet that actually fall in love. In fact, we're the only beings that love. Animals have instincts but we can actually love forever—we're an amazing species. We've got this ability to love and be loved and I think the human being wants to love, be loved, and be happy.

I ask a lot of people, "How many happy people do you know?" Not too many, because most of us are in the animal brain just trying to survive the day. When we're trying to survive the day and we're at work, we don't really want to be there. Work becomes a four-letter word and customers become a nuisance. I've actually worked with customer service representatives who say, "If it wasn't for the customer, I'd do a great job, but they keep getting in the way." Well, they are supposed to! They are customers.

When you're in the animal brain you perceive everything as hard work—everything is a problem and those people are out to get you so get them first! You think, "I won't make eye contact. I'll be gruff on the phone. I'll just do my job and hope to get home to the cave where I can relax."

Wright

So how do I stay in the human brain as long as possible?

Gee

We do what we call "affirming your day." We've discovered that very successful people know that they're going to have a great day, even if it's going to suck, because they know that's what they are capable of doing—they can take anything and make it better. This is how it works. When you get up in the morning you stand in front of the mirror and you talk to yourself, because you're talking to yourself anyway. When you're in the animal brain it doesn't even like what it sees in the mirror—you're never quite up to it—you're either too short, too tall, too fat, too thin, big nose, no hair, too much hair, whatever it is. The human being brain thinks you're actually gorgeous, that you're talented, fabulous, and amazing. We affirm our day every day—we stand in front of the mirror and we say, "You and I [the "you" here is the animal, The "I" is the human being] just today," because I know you can't do a five-year plan. Say, "You and I today are going to be amazing. We're gorgeous, talented, fabulous, caring, sharing, giving, and loving, just for today. Just today you and I are going to be great! We're going to work, this is what we're going to do, and we're going to have a great day, even if people are rude to us and even if the manager says something that we don't agree with—we are going to be amazing because we can be. So please get in the shower and sing your heart out!"

We demand that everybody who goes through our training sing in the shower every morning. There've been studies done all around the world about this. When people sing in the shower every morning they always feel good afterwards—it's just a state of mind. We get people to affirm their day every day and sing in the shower and switch their brain back into the human one. That gives them the power to realize, I don't have to be at the mercy of the day, I don't have to be at the mercy of my boss, I don't have to be at the mercy of this rude customer, I can still be amazing with them—when they walk away they can say, "Wow that person was great!"

Wright

So actually staying in the human brain is a choice.

Gee

Absolutely. The problem we have, you see, is that I can make choices all day long. If I want to be depressed, oh, I can be depressed in a second. I can just think of the thing and it knocks me down for the whole day, or I can say, "Wait a minute! Being depressed doesn't work. I'd rather be alive, ready to rock and roll! I'll switch back up again, thank you."

Wright

When we think about business and how we treat our customers, what about that old adage that says, "The customer is always right." Does that still hold true?

Gee

Well yes it does, David. It does actually hold true. It's how we handle it and how we manifest that truth that the customer is always right, even when they're completely wrong. We've got to look at not being at the mercy of the customer. It's still okay to be able to tell people, "No, this is not the way we do business" and, "No, you can't have that," and, "No, this is our policy and procedure."

The customer is always right because they are the customer, so they always demand whatever it is they want. They want to get what they want even if it's outrageous. Our job is to connect with them at a different level so that our customers can be educated about what we will do and what we won't do for them.

We've done surveys with customers—with different organizations—and it's amazing how many of them really don't know what that company will and will not do for them. Of course their expectation level increases exponentially so that when something goes wrong they're terribly disappointed because their expectation level is so high. Our job, as customer service providers and managers and VPs, is to let everybody know exactly what we can do and what we can't do. We constantly have to keep re-educating customers because they forget. So, yes they're always right and our job is to make sure that they understand there are certain things that they can and cannot have.

Wright

When the customer is angry, how do you handle that sort of situation?

Gee

Well, it's okay, because when they're angry they're coming from the animal brain. When people are angry they will literally say and do anything. As we all know—because we've all been angry—we've said the most upsetting things to people that at the time we meant, because we were angry, we were in the animal brain and we wanted to strike out. It's flight-or-fight—well I'm going to fight you now so I'm going to say nasty things about you. Usually we regret what we've said almost as soon as we've said them; but it's too late, we've said them. Now in that situation I have to understand that I have to stay in the human brain. This is important because if I connect in the animal brain, now there are two animals fighting and the customer animal will always win. In addition, you don't want to be fighting each other. It's not a pretty sight and we end up losing the customer.

I stay in the human brain if they're angry. My job is to bring them back into the human brain by just being with them, understanding the pain that they're going through, and not taking anything they say personally. If I take it personally I'll slip immediately back into the animal brain and then we're having a fight again.

We talk to people about not taking things personally because when someone is angry, they're saying things they don't really mean. They would never dream of talking that way if they were in the human brain. When they are angry, negative stuff comes out. We don't take it personally. They can say anything they want to me—they can use my name, call me an idiot, horrendous or say, "We hate you!" That's fine. My job is to connect with them and help them, then they can go from the animal to the human brain and people will actually walk away saying, "Wow! That person was amazing!"

Wright

So how do you handle stress in your life?

Gee

I accept the fact that it's going to be there. Technology is this most amazing thing that's opened up boundaries and allowed us to be global. Of course, the side effect of that is there's a lot of stress now because everything's instant. The *U.S. News & World Report* magazine doesn't even call us human beings anymore; they call us consumers, because that's what we are. We want everything and we want it immediately. We don't really want to pay for it and we want to get upset if it's not exactly right because the animal brain comes out again.

Now, when we are here with people and connected with people there's a magic that happens that transcends all of those things and allows us to be really where we need to be with them. When we're doing all of this we've got to understand, "I know I'm going to have stress because that's just the nature of life." As soon as I feel stress coming on I can say, "Excellent! Oh, that's stress. Now I've tried that before, okay. How do I have power over stress and the energy that stress creates, and turn it into a positive thing? How can I can take the stress and relieve it in a way that allows me to be open and caring again with what I need to do in my life?" I need to think that way instead of letting stress get past the optimum level and I get freaked out, worried, upset, depressed, miserable, etc. Handling stress properly means accepting that stress is there, looking at it and then using energy and power it creates in a good way.

Wright

That's great information, especially about the three parts of the brain. How can this information be applied to my personal life?

Gee

What we'd like you and everyone else to be able to do with that is start affirming your day. Start to look at how you're treating people. Look at whether you're really being at your best or have you slipped into your animal brain again?

In my personal life I want to make sure that the relationship I have with my wife is an amazing one. That means that I have to get out of the way, stop taking things personally, and connect with her because we're the only creatures on the planet that love. I ask people, "When you were in love, what was it like?" Everybody says the same thing and I've asked this in Hong Kong, Singapore, Brazil, Argentina, Venezuela and Europe. Everybody says—it was great to be in love—it was wonderful.

I ask, "How was your life when you were in love?"

"What do you mean my life?"

"What was it like going to work? What was it like being with other people?"

"Everything was great!"

When you're in love everything is great. How long does it last? Then we get the answer, "Oh, well, not too long." Why not? Well then reality creeps in. Oh, you mean the animal brain creeps in. The animal doesn't even want you to be happy, it just wants you to survive so it starts looking for problems. Suddenly that wonderful person you fell in love with and the very same attributes that you fell in love with about that person are now becoming problems. Isn't it crazy what we do to ourselves!

Our job is to remember, to remember, to remember that we're in love. It starts with me, I have to love myself—not in a sycophantic way—but in a way that says you're an amazing human being and you're capable of doing anything that you set your mind to.

What do human beings really want to do? I think the reason that we're on the planet is to be of service to each other—human beings need other human beings. But how do I connect with as many other human beings as I can so I basically shine my light so it allows other people to shine theirs? It starts with me. My personal life is affected strongly by this whole process, as is my work life.

Wright

Well, interesting, very interesting. I've learned a lot here today. You've given me some things that I already had been thinking about but now I've got some handles to put on them. Maybe I can consider some of these things and even change for the better!

Gee

Absolutely! You know, the thing I've learned is I actually can't change—Jeff Gee is Jeff Gee. I popped out of the oven the way I am— my upbringing, DNA, this is Jeff Gee—but I can make choices now. I want to make great choices now. I want to really have a loving, happy life. To do that I've got to stop talking to myself about how everybody's out to get me, and these people looked at me wrong, and that wasn't necessary, and that was rude. I have to just stop all of that and connect with this amazing human spirit that will allow me to connect with everybody and be amazing all the time.

Wright

Well, I want to thank you for taking so much time out of your day here to answer these questions. This has been really helpful and I hope the readers of this book really delve into some of these techniques and some of these issues that you've talked about.

Gee

Excellent, thank you David!

Wright

Today we've been talking to Jeff Gee about such things as customer service and making great choices to have great days. We've also learned about the three sections of the brain and I think I, for one, have got some thinking to do about how to use that information.

Jeff, thank you so much for being with us today on *Pillars of Success!*

Gee

It's a pleasure, thank you!

About The Author

JEFF GEE was brought to the U.S. from the U.K. in 1983 by a multinational company to improve sales and employee productivity. In two years, he increased U.S. sales by 60 percent. During that process, Jeff realized there was a real need to provide amazing customer service and excellence to corporate America; that was the beginning of MJ Learning.

Featured on major television networks, Jeff has shared his expertise and knowledge on customer loyalty to millions of viewers. Consultant to Fortune 500 companies worldwide, NSA member, and renowned author; Jeff gets people to take responsibility and be their personal best every day.

Jeff Gee

McNeil & Johnson Corporation

24089 N Forest Drive

Lake Zurich, Illinois 60047

Phone: 847-438-9366

E-mail: coach@mjlearning.com

www.mjlearning.com

Chapter Two

GENERAL ALEXANDER HAIG

THE INTERVIEW

David E. Wright (Wright)

General Haig really needs no introduction as he is among the most decorated military and civilian figures of our times. In addition to his military accomplishments, General Haig has held a number of key positions in political and business leadership and presently serves as Chairman of Worldwide Associates, Inc., an international advisory firm based in Washington, D.C. He is a senior advisor to United Technologies Corporation, a corporation for which he served as President and Chief Operating Officer, 1979–1981. In addition, he is the host of the weekly television program, *World Business Review*.

General Haig is perhaps best known as United States Secretary of State under President Ronald Reagan, appointed by the President-elect and confirmed by the United States Senate. However, many are familiar with General Haig's reputation as a paragon of statesmanship with the mental and tactical genius befitting a four-star general, and the consummate diplomacy of a master negotiator at the highest levels of the public and private sectors.

General Haig, welcome to *Pillars of Success*.

Alexander M. Haig, Jr. (Haig)

Thank you very much. It's great to be with you David.

Wright

Before we get into some of the questions I have prepared, knowing how you worked for President Reagan, his funeral was very difficult for the nation. How did you view the funeral?

Haig

In hindsight, now that the emotional side of the funeral has faded, I think one of the event's greatest satisfactions to me is that the President was so widely recognized for his accomplishments as a leader of our nation. That recognition was universal regardless of political party. Some of the positive tone in the liberal press was unfortunately a product of their recognizing that critical or unacceptable analyses would not be welcomed by the majority of American readers. That's true of the networks as well. So they were "on their good behavior" after a few forays in the opposite direction.

Having said that, I think really it gave us all an opportunity to reflect on the great accomplishments of this wonderful leader and the superb achievements he realized during his brief eight-year incumbency.

Wright

You know, I felt really good about the entire funeral process. I thought honoring him that way was something I think the American people really, really wanted to do. But I did read two or three columns that offended me that so soon after his passing they would write negative articles about the President.

Haig

I had one interrogation on CNN where the interrogator said, in effect, "You left the President, so you obviously had differences. Would you tell us what his shortcomings were?"

I replied, "If I thought he had shortcomings, which I didn't, you'd be the last person I'd give them to. Furthermore, at this time, the question is very inappropriate in any event."

Wright

Well, great!

Haig

And so he got rather apologetic. I was naughty on that occasion.

Wright

Well, you deserved to be. Most men and women of my generation are familiar with your career, General. We watched you advance in the military and go on to play a vital role in the Vietnam ceasefire and the return of the U.S. prisoners of war. We remember the part you played in President Nixon's historic opening to China. We've watched you on the world stage as Secretary of State under Ronald Reagan, after your distinguished service as NATO Commander. There may be, however, a segment of our population that does not understand the depth of your contribution to the United States and the world for that matter. Before we move into a discussion focused on the topic of leadership, would you look back over your career and tell us how you feel about the life you've lived? In other words, what aspect of your life gives you the most satisfaction?

Haig

I think, basically, I look back with gratitude to the Almighty for having exposed me to the great array of historic events I participated in—from the first day of my military service, with my close exposure to Douglas MacArthur in Tokyo and later during the Korean War including the landing in Inchon and finally evacuation on a stretcher in late 1951 following the Chinese Intervention. In addition to the Korean War, I witnessed every major historic event up until quite recently. I participated in the Cuban missile crisis at the highest level in the Pentagon and in Vietnam where I commanded a battalion of infantry and a brigade of infantry of the First Infantry Division in '66 and '67 at the height of the war. Beyond that, of course, serving as President Reagan's first Secretary of State, as well as my time with Presidents Nixon, Ford, and Carter.

But I think I really look back mostly at my beginnings, and that was to be part of a family unit in which we had strong Christian convictions under a father who was a high Episcopalian—a very ardent one—and a mother who was a devout Roman Catholic. They say, "never the twain shall meet," but in this case it did! As a result, my father became a Catholic and was really the most devout of any member of the family. He instilled strong Christian convictions in our entire family. My mother lived by them, as well, showing great respect and love for her husband who died when she was in her thirties.

I was only nine years old. He was also an extremely successful lawyer in Philadelphia, so our life's expectations suddenly changed dramatically.

At that time my mother didn't even know how to keep a checkbook. She had to take charge of a family that had more debt than assets because my father had been such a generous provider. Nevertheless, she educated her only daughter in the law graduating from the University of Pennsylvania. My sister became a very successful lawyer. My younger brother became a Jesuit priest, a highly regarded educator, and a nuclear and astronautical physicist. He was also the President of two Jesuit universities and is still teaching at Loyola University in Baltimore.

Of course my greatest joy these days is anchored to my wonderful wife, Patricia, who like my mother had to fill in for me because of my frequent absences and the outrageous hours I keep. She did a superb job and today I have three wonderful children and eight grandchildren.

My oldest son is like my father and sister—a lawyer. He is working with me in my many varied business activities. My second son is a best-selling author who has just completed his fifth novel that will be released by Warner Books early next year. He was a West Point trained infantry officer and was one of the Army's top strategic planners. Finally, my daughter, Barbara, is a senior executive in the National Endowment for Democracy located in our nation's Capital. She has dedicated her life to the promotion of democratic values worldwide.

Wright

Hmmm, that's a varied career.

Haig

As World War II was approaching, as a youth I saw the military as my best hope for the future. From my early years, I also had a very keen interest in national security and foreign affairs. Then, as today, our service academies provided great opportunities for young men and today for women, including those who come from less than affluent backgrounds. I was admitted to West Point and graduated in 1947. I look back on those experiences with the utmost satisfaction.

I am, of course, also thankful for the opportunity to be a witness in such a span of history, working for Presidents Kennedy, Johnson, Nixon, Ford, Carter, and Reagan. That's six presidents, four of whom called me by my first name. I think few Americans have had more rewarding experiences.

Wright

You know, of all of your accomplishments, I'm certainly impressed with one that I hadn't realized before. You were actually on General MacArthur's staff, were you not?

Haig

Indeed I was. I worked with his Chief of Staff, Lt. General "Ned" Almond, and worked almost daily with General MacArthur himself. I frequently carried papers back and forth from his office and briefed him on the battlefield situation each evening during the early weeks of the Korean War. I saw firsthand an individual who I consider to be one of the finest leaders I have ever known.

Wright

Yes.

Haig

Few people appreciate the lessons one learns from close contact with such men. I sat just outside the conference room door, during the meeting between Douglas MacArthur and the Joint Chiefs of Staff, who had been sent by President Truman to Tokyo to tell MacArthur he should not execute the Inchon Landing. During this meeting, each service chief in one way or another said that they couldn't support the operation. The one who was the least negative was Admiral Sherman, the Chief of Naval Operations. MacArthur sat there silently during each of their presentations. When they finished he stood up, carefully put his pipe in the ashtray before him, looked directly at the assembled leaders, and said, "Gentlemen, I will land at Inchon on the fifteenth of September or you will have a new commander in the Far East." He then slowly walked out of the room. The opposition completely collapsed under what I would describe as the towering character of a rare individual who would rather be right than simply keep his job.

Wright

Right!

Haig

And that's a very important principle of leadership forgotten so often by many of our contemporary leaders.

Wright

We're discussing leadership principles from a variety of perspectives today. I'd be very interested in hearing your thoughts on the character of a leader. Do you think people are born hardwired to be good leaders or can it be taught?

Haig

This is a classic and a very relevant question. I've thought about it many times. My answer would be *both*. Some are gifted with strong leadership traits and certainly MacArthur and Ronald Reagan fit that mold in every respect. Some, however, have acquired their talents through study and diligence. They recognize that they can learn and develop leadership principles if they study and analyze those traits demonstrated by the more gifted. Both the gifted and the less gifted can always improve their leadership skills and seek to do so by constant attention to building sound leadership traits. This is what our service academies attempt to accomplish. It is also what all of our schools should teach and emphasize, especially in professions where leadership is essential.

Wright

You know, with the recent corporate scandals still fresh in our memories, a million people today think that we're experiencing a leadership crisis in America. I've been thinking about how different America was in past generations. Fathers led their families with firm discipline and many men attended military school as youngsters. Our national leaders presented a model that most men and women admired. Even the wars we fought in the past fostered great leaders. Things are very different now.

General Haig, do you have any thoughts or theories about the status of leadership in America today?

Haig

I think, David, we've all thought about this as we watched some of the modern tendencies emerge. There are many complex contributors to this in my view. One, above all, would be the breakdown of the family unit in America. Sometimes that's not the choice of the parents involved but the product of necessity in modern society. In these cases frequently it results in failure to instill traditional family values and principles. But there are other factors.

One, of course, is today's educational process. History has become a lost art. Political theory is seldom taught. For its students the study of political theory refines the proven universal principles of human conduct and behavior. Take, for example, some of our liberal education today. It seems to focus less on teaching classical values highlighted in the study of political theory, and emphasizes what works at the moment in a purely pragmatic sense. That approach emphasizes what's of contemporary utility rather than what's right.

The second major contributor, I think, is the explosion in information sciences and its impact, some of which is good, but some of which has had a deleterious impact on modern society. It has created the "modern populist" in government in business, in education, and in other leadership positions around America.

Populism has produced the fellow who gets up every morning, puts his finger to the wind, and says, "What's going to make me popular today?" He then rushes to deliver. Too many leaders today are populists, especially among contemporary political leaders. This style also affects their subordinates. It has produced a character trait that leads them to tell the boss what he thinks the boss *wishes* to hear rather than what the boss *should* hear. We see a lot of that in government today. And that's why presidents who become isolated by the sycophants within their staffs, risk not knowing what's really going on in the country.

Wright

I recently had an opportunity to go into the attic and I found my old University of Tennessee catalog I got when I started in 1957. I looked at the course outlines for the four years in my college education and I compared it with the ones today. I mean, badminton and ping-pong just doesn't seem to make it, you know? You get credits for the strangest things in our universities today and you don't have to take as many hours.

Haig

I agree with you. You know, I think back to Winston Churchill. After the end of World War II he was asked by a group of students, "Mr. Prime Minister, how did you learn statecraft?"

He replied, "Read history, young man. Read history, because only through a knowledge of history can you begin to open the secrets of statecraft." We have forgotten that in today's educational system.

Wright
If you don't mind, I'd like to go back to your time on active duty in Vietnam. Were there significant events that took place while you were overseas fighting for America that shaped you as a leader or influenced your effectiveness as a political statesman for example?

Haig
Unquestionably. There is nothing more intense than having responsibility for the lives of young men and women in battle. I think one of the characteristics resulting from that experience was the *requirement to communicate*. I mean the need to communicate continuously, time permitting. If you do that as a military leader especially, but also as a corporate leader or a political leader, then those you are responsible for will tend to follow you when time doesn't permit you to communicate. They will recognize that, were time available, you would explain everything because they learned to count on you to do that.

Another principle is to remember that *a flawed policy adopted on time is better than a perfect policy decided too late*. Perhaps most importantly you must be able to separate the problems from the facts. Take, for example, those who have been critical of what they think the policy of "globalism" is. The truth is that globalism *is not a policy*; rather, *it's a fact*. Today we live in a world that is increasingly interdependent, politically, and economically and in every other sense of the word, even in moral and security terms. In sum, you must learn to accept and to work with *facts* while you must solve problems with appropriate policies. So, what our leaders must do is learn to work with globalism and to do so in a way that best suits the interests of our people. These are the things that combat experience taught me. But they also come from government and business experience.

Finally, too frequently among some of the six presidents I've served at close range, loyalty seemed to be a question of "what did you do for me today?" The real obligation of loyalty is to remember that it goes down more importantly than it goes up. Oddly enough (and you'll be surprised at this), the President I knew well who was most heavily imbued with the principle of loyalty was Richard Nixon. There was never a day that I spoke with that man—and I did so every day—that he didn't inquire about my family, or apologize for placing me in the position he did during the height of Watergate. In general, he was the most solicitous of all of the presidents I served. It is very important for leaders to remember that *loyalty must go down as well as go up*.

Wright

You mentioned Nixon. If I could, and if he were alive, I'd vote for him again today. I think he was a great president. Many Americans have become fans of the hit television show, *The West Wing*.

Haig

Oh, boy!

Wright

I find the behind-the-scenes aspect of the show fascinating. You spent many years in the White House serving Presidents Nixon, Ford, and Reagan. Your role as Chief of Staff in 1973 is particularly relevant to today's discussion on leadership. Are there lessons that you learned serving with the top decision-makers in the free world that our readers can apply to their role as business leaders?

Haig

I think frequently it is important to avoid what I call the exclusive preoccupation with expediency. You can't always look for something that will chase the wolf away today. You also must think about the long-term interests of the corporation or any institution. Sometimes this requires you to do things that are very unpopular. Take Mr. Reagan's Presidency, where he had to start out and create the impression of a two-gun cowboy. He knew that our hostages in Iran had inflicted a mortal blow on American credibility throughout the Middle East and he was determined that he was going to obtain their release. During the transition then-Secretary of State Ed Muskey came to me and asked if the Democrats could get the President-elect's okay to continue the negotiations with Tehran for another six months. And I said, "Well, I haven't had a chance to talk to President Reagan and I'll do so immediately, but, if you need your answer now, you can tell the Iranians that the President-elect has made it clear to me that with the first moment of his presidency, if those prisoners have not been released, it will be an entirely new ballgame."

I then rushed over to the Blair House to talk to the President to be sure he was comfortable with what I had said. He looked at me, smiled and said, "Al, I think you were a little bit too soft." You'll recall that those prisoners were released minutes before he commenced his Inaugural Address.

That began a process of re-establishing American credibility. Our attacks on Libya, Panama, Grenada, and the other actions he took early on created a whole new and greatly needed respect for his foreign policies. Before his inauguration, we had discussed the fact that the Soviets were in an advanced state of decay. Unfortunately, they also believed America was soft and wouldn't fight if need be. The credibility that President Reagan established in those early days of his presidency enabled us years later to witness the collapse of the Soviet system and the liberation of Eastern Europe without a shot being fired. This is the same challenge we as a nation face in the struggle with global terrorism today. We simply must re-establish America's credibility in the struggle with Islamic extremism.

Wright

I can remember when the prisoners were freed, and I remember the pride that I had just as a citizen. And I remember that I laid all of it right at the feet of Ronald Reagan—I gave him the mental credit for that.

Haig

You were absolutely right. And another characteristic he showed at that time was not to rush over to Europe and take full credit for it, but to ask former President Carter to go to Europe and receive our prisoners in Germany. So he wasn't thirsting for the credit.

Wright

Are you at liberty to share one or two specific historical examples of when you and those around you in the White House were forced to exercise extreme leadership qualities under pressure?

Haig

One always is subjective on such matters. And the first thing I'd like to touch upon was the day President Reagan was shot. The Cabinet and staff members were assembled in the White House Situation Room. All knew the President was seriously wounded, but after checking with the Chief of Staff who was at the hospital, we decided not to invoke the 25th Amendment and not to consider designating the Vice President as Acting President. This was a unanimous Cabinet group decision (later confirmed by the Vice President).

Subsequently, we learned the Secretary of Defense had altered our nuclear alert status from a normal "DEFCON" to a higher level of alert, which could easily be picked up by both the press and the Soviets. We also observed on national television the acting press secretary telling the press assembled in the White House that he didn't know if we had changed our alert status or who was administering the government with the President wounded and Vice President in the air and out of town. I then rushed to the pressroom with the National Security Advisor to be sure friend and foe knew we had a functioning government, especially since the Secretary of Defense had changed our nuclear alert, which was probably known to the Soviets with very dangerous potential consequences.

During the press conference I told the press (and friends and foe) that our government was being administered by a Cabinet Group under me as the Senior Cabinet member and that we were on our normal alert status. Just afterwards, Dan Rather attacked me on CBS television claiming I thought I was next in line to be President. This had been triggered by a senior member of the White House Staff and has been the subject of a recent totally inaccurate television film. Recently, I learned that before that fateful press conference, Soviet nuclear forces were at their highest state of alert, but returned to normal just after my presentation.

I still get lambasted for that pressroom appearance. Believe me, under similar circumstances, I would do it again. As I've gone around the world, leaders in many capitols have said to me, "Thank God you did what you did."

Wright

Well, that was my take on it. Of course, I've heard it a thousand times since you said it, but I took a different view. I thought, "Thank God he's in charge."

Haig

Dan Rather had a cute way of editing what I said then; bringing in two professors from colleges in New York City to confirm that I didn't know the line of succession.

Wright

They were giving us a civics lesson.

Haig

But, as usual, you always have to remember that the press sometimes is rather evil in its own right. More often than not, however, it is triggered by some insidious character right in the president's own family—leakers with other axes to grind.

Now, the second incident worth noting was the Christmas bombing during the Vietnam War. You recall it was very controversial, and that we had bombed Hanoi and Haiphong, using B-52s against massive opposition from the Congress. Before long they were threatening impeachment and removal of the President. Even the President's most ardent supporters within his staff finally caved in and said to the President, "You've got to cease." At the same time the North Vietnamese blinked and said they wanted to resume the talks in Paris. I was opposed and urged the President to continue to bomb until we had an agreement that Hanoi would totally withdraw from South Vietnam. Unfortunately, the political pressure was overwhelming, and the President was forced to halt the bombing and resume negotiations. I have said to other Presidents since then, "Mr. President, better you be impeached for doing what is right for our people."

I hope that people will understand that the pressures the United States is under today in the Iraq War are not unprecedented. There are those who are now suggesting that we get out of Iraq. They should remember: we didn't win a battle in World War II until over a year after we entered it. We lost an armored division at Kasserine Pass and Anzio was a disaster. There were many other failures as well; but we didn't have the American press or political opponents condemning the President, calling him a liar, a cheat, and a dissembler. I am confident we are doing the right thing in the war on terrorism, and history will confirm that. Of course, we have done some of it in a flawed way, which is not uncommon. We have to be more patient.

What is now at stake is the belief among many Americans, aided and abetted by the liberal press in America, that because there were flaws in the way we did the right thing, we shouldn't have done the right thing in the first place. That's the great danger we are now confronting.

Wright

Because many of the old international walls have come down in the past twenty years, some Americans don't remember how extraordinary it was when President Nixon visited China in February of 1972. You were instrumental in making this trip a success, which leads me to the topic of negotiating, strategy, and détente in relationship to leadership. What lessons can you share with American business professionals based on your experience in world politics?

Haig

A very important lesson is patience. We spent almost two years with the great skills of Henry Kissinger and all of the National Security Council team sending signals back and forth to China, some of which were rebuffed. Now, we all know Ronald Reagan was indispensable to the victory in the Cold War, but he didn't win that war single-handedly. That was a process that was inevitable over time because of the internal contradictions and flawed character of Marxist Leninism. Everybody who has studied history knew that, and certainly Ronald Reagan above all knew that. When I first discussed the Soviet Union with him, he said he also agreed with me that the Soviets were failing. He also noted, as history confirms, that when totalitarian regimes are in an advanced state of decay, they are the most dangerous because they lash out seeking to divert the peoples' attention. And so he said, "First, Al, we have to re-establish American credibility," which had been so damaged by the previous administration due to the hostage crisis and other mistakes. This, as I said, dominated his handling of the hostage crisis with Iran.

We also had Libya. We had Panama. We had Grenada. As a result, Mr. Gorbechev realized that he was not only confronting failure, but also a resolute new America that was willing to fight for its values. Ronald Reagan did this by his firm policies and clearheaded decision-making. He brought about the end of the Cold War without firing a shot. We should be careful that we don't claim more than we've earned and that we keep that victory in focus because in the process of over-simplifying, we don't make the late President look nearly as thoughtful as he really was.

Wright

So this was a matter of teamwork over many years?

Haig

Many years. And it was contributed to by almost every American president. Some did it successfully like President Reagan; some did it less than successfully. We did it by staying together and by using détente as a shield in the nuclear age, together with the recognition that communism would ultimately fail of its own internal contradictions. Reagan also realized that negotiations were far better than a nuclear war. Happily, our leaders managed to stand together with those who shared our values, especially in Europe and NATO, to unify and create the coalition of deterrence that brought about a victory for all.

Wright

General Haig, will you tell us how you were using your leadership experience during this exciting phase of your career? I understand you advise a number of corporate leaders. What kind of impact do you have in the private sector?

Haig

Like most human endeavors, sometimes I'm successful; sometimes I'm not heard, and sometimes it's good I'm not. I think the two most important things I can reflect on would be that I believed years ago the world is changing and we must work with these facts or changes. The world was becoming more interdependent or, as we call it today, more global, and that the future of the corporations and American businesses require expanding our horizons into international trade and commerce. Again, that this was a fact and not a policy choice to be made or rejected.

Wright

I noted that you have had significant influence in academic circles having served in a variety of leadership roles for schools such as Princeton, Tulane, and Yale, and such think-tanks as the Foreign Policy Research Institute in Philadelphia. You also lecture at colleges and universities across America. Do you believe our universities are doing an acceptable job preparing men and women to lead?

Haig

First let me say this in general: We have great standards, especially in higher education. America is the best in the world by far, and that's why foreign students are streaming to our shores despite political differences. But again, I would say there is not a sufficient amount of attention to the wisdom of the ages, which only comes through an intimate knowledge of political theory. All our quests for knowledge are quests for the truth, and the truth is very hard to arrive at in a universal sense because of the constantly changing environment in which these values mature. So we've got to get back to a point where we don't just teach what the professors might think is currently successful by looking at the world as a snapshot in time. That to me is the most serious educational flaw we face today in both lower and higher education. All of the other things we've talked about—family, values, and principles—are, of course, an intimate part of this need. So, I guess I'm a little old fashioned—I believe in the lessons of yesterday.

Wright

You know, I talked to one of your associates earlier this week and quite frankly just asked him, "Is it going to be easy to get along with General Haig? Am I going to be smart enough to talk to this man?"

He laughed and said, "Yes. What kind of questions are you going to ask him?"

I told him a few, and he said, "You really need to ask him about his nine commandments of leadership," which I had no knowledge of.

I hope I'm not taking you by surprise, but I would love for you to share these nine commandments of leadership for our readers.

Haig

All right. Well, David, I'll keep these short because I've given you some of the examples already in what we've said.

The first, of course, would be *integrity*—a leader must mean what he says and say what he means.

I suppose the second rule would be what we've already discussed rather ad nauseam and that's *loyalty*. Good leaders know it goes down as well as up.

Rule three I talked about, *communication*. I won't say any more other than the fact that if you communicate, you lead. If you just order in martinet fashion, it's very hard to lead except by fear; that's not the way traditional American leadership excels.

Rule four is *follow and demonstrate the courage of your convictions* as MacArthur did when he said, "I either land in Inchon because I know the theater better than you fellows, and it's the right thing to do. If you disagree, get yourself another leader." I have resigned from three presidencies on principle, and I would do it again.

The fifth is to *welcome dissent*. Usually, whether it was in business or in the military, I bring in the implementers, including those who are on the cutting edge of implementation. That usually involves going down to the younger people. If you listen only to the older or more senior executives you risk talking to the sycophants. So always try to get down on to the floor at the cutting edge of your business whether it's a shop floor or whether it's a marketing structure where the guys are in the trenches, so to speak. Talk to them regularly, listen to them, and shape your policies in accordance with their hands-on experience.

Rule six is *work hard*. There's nothing for nothing in this world. But also remember that old adage of, "All work and no play makes Jack a dull boy." So be sure your people understand that and pursue policies that provide exercise and recreation.

I've talked about rule seven—*decide carefully but in a timely fashion*. I've belabored that already too much, but it's very important.

And of course, rule eight I've talked about already and that's *avoid populism*. Don't be a finger-in-the-wind leader.

And finally rule nine is *professionalism*. We haven't talked about that, but it's critically important for whatever discipline you work in that you know your business, which comes from constant reading, constant study, and constant interface with other experts in the field to be sure you know the latest thinking, the latest developments, as well as the principles that guide the discipline you're involved with.

Wright

Boy, those are great. Our readers and I thank you. General Haig, our time together has really been a sincere pleasure for me. Before we let you go, do you have any closing remarks for our readers?

Haig

I think the most important thing is to be very leery of instantaneous press reporting in the modern world. We've seen it in instance after instance. The most recent was that there was no connection whatsoever between Saddam Hussein and al Qaeda when the facts are really to the contrary as the 9/11 Commission concluded. Every scholarly assessment I've read, including the most recent, *The Secret History of the Iraq War*, by Yossef Bodansky, presents a remarkable confirmation of the interrelationship of all terrorist activities. The father of terrorism was none other than the Marxist-Leninist Soviet Russia. They're the ones who taught all of the techniques and principles the terrorists are adhering to today.

So these are things I think are the most important. Also, stay behind our leaders and have the vision to recognize these dangers. This is a global conflict. It's going to go on for a long, long time. There are going to be setbacks as well as victories. But ultimately this great nation, if we work in concert with our allies abroad—those who share our values—we are going to triumph and the world will be the beneficiary.

Wright

As I stated in the beginning, it has been an honor to welcome you, General Alexander Haig, to *Pillars of Success*. You just don't know how much I appreciate the time you've spent with me here today, and I'm sure our readers are going to get a tremendous amount of information from this. Thank you so much, sir.

Haig

Thank you very much.

About The Author

General Haig is a voice of authority and experience, having served as White House Chief of Staff for President Nixon, NATO Commander (1974–1979), Secretary of State (1981–1982), corporate leader, scholar, teacher, diplomat, and military leader. He is host of his own weekly television program, *World Business Review,* and is a regular commentator on the war on terrorism, Iraq, and North Korea, having been seen recently on programs such as *Hardball* and *Hannity and Colmes*.

General Haig is the author of two books: *Caveat: Realism, Reagan* and *Foreign Policy* (1984), and his autobiography, *Inner Circles: How America Changed the World: A Memoir* (1992). He is married to the former Patricia Fox. The Haigs are the parents of three children and have eight grandchildren.

Chapter Three

LOUIS MONSOUR

THE INTERVIEW

David Wright (Wright)

Today we're talking with Louis Monsour. He is President and Chief Executive Officer of IBS Enterprises, Inc. He has nine years of experience in asset protection, legal tax reduction, corporate credit and finance, and overall business consulting. Mr. Monsour strives at educating the entrepreneur and current business owner in the areas of asset protection, legal tax savings, establishing proper corporate credit, and taking on business ventures which include real estate, international trade, and the entertainment industry. Mr. Monsour has extensive experience in law, real estate, and as an investor and consultant. He also has experience in the entertainment industry. He worked for four years at the second largest law firm in the United States, O'Melveny and Myers, as a paralegal.

While attending law school he moved on to Universal Feature Legal Department, Studios USA television, DreamWorks Business Affairs, Disney's International Acquisition and Distribution, and Universal Television. Mr. Monsour has a Bachelor of Science degree in business with emphasis on communication, finance, and real estate from the University of Southern California.

Although he is a law school graduate he does not practice law. He enjoys consulting and has clients from various industries such as entertainment, real estate investors, contractors, and high-tech companies. In addition to running the business and his many involvements with various industries, Mr. Monsour was a professor at Westwood College where he taught business ethics, criminal law, and criminal procedure among other subjects. Currently he hosts the *Make It and Keep It* hour on KTSA 550AM or www.KTSA.com on Saturdays from 1:00 until 2:00 PM (CST). He is married with three boys of ten, eight, and two years of age.

Louis, welcome to *Pillars of Success*.

Louis Monsour

Thank you, glad to be here.

Wright

So, tell us how and why you began your business.

Monsour

I've been working with corporations for quite some time but the way I got into the asset protection side of business is when someone decided to sue my father. My father owned a gas station and a garage. He took pity on a man who was sleeping in his car parked in my Dad's parking lot. My father gave him food, clothing, paid for medication when he was sick—the whole nine yards. One day this man (I hesitate to call him a gentleman) filed a lawsuit against my father for $100,000. He filed with the Employment Development Department saying that my father owed him wages as well as overtime. To say the least that took us back a bit. Whoa! What's going on?

We went to the Employment Development Department and brought in our witnesses saying that this guy never worked at my father's business. We brought in people he talked to saying he never worked there. We then went on to arbitration and then on to court. Before we even started, the judge looked at him and he said, "Son I recommend you settle because although I can't throw it out, you're not going to win this case." Then the judge looked at me and said, "You're going to win this case but it's going to cost you some money so you might want to consider your options as far as cost." To make a long story, short, we settled for a $100.00 off of a $100,000 lawsuit. It was going to cost me $500 to $600 to file the next set of papers! That was my door into the asset protection—somebody thought, "Hey, this man owns his own business, I'll make some money."

Wright

Your company slogan has been, "The small business development company." What makes you different from everyone else?

Monsour

We're different because we don't establish a company for the heck of establishing one. If you want to form a corporation we sit down with you and we find out what it is you want to do, and what your plan is for one year, two years, five years, and ten years down the road—that's a development plan. It's not, "Oh, I want to incorporate. Well, fill out this paper and we'll take care of it for you."

There are a lot of people in this industry, as with just about any industry (especially law since that's what I studied), where a few rotten apples can ruin the entire barrel. We're in a business where it's easy to manipulate this information and to scam, not only other creditors, but also the government, your spouse—you name it. So we investigate. We don't set up corporations for people who are simply trying to illegally beat the system. We do it to legally protect a person's assets, and legally reduce taxes.

We're in the business of empowering businesses to succeed and the only way we can do that is by doing it legitimately, all in-house. I guess you could call us the "Wal-Mart" of asset protection, or incorporation, or business development. We take what the small business development center does, what the SBA does, what an incorporating company does, and what a lot of the consultants out there running free do, and we bring it all under one roof at a fraction of the cost.

Wright

You mentioned asset protection, tax reduction, and corporate credit. Just what are they and how important are they exactly?

Monsour

Well, as I explained with that opening story, asset protection was very important to my father at the time. We were in the process of incorporating when my father was sued so, had we lost that lawsuit and had this man won a $100,000 judgment, my father would have been in trouble. At the time my father only had about $50,000 in the account so the next thing the court would have done would have been to take his car, his house, or any other personal stocks and investments he had to satisfy that judgment.

I find it very irresponsible for anyone looking to go into business without having protection, especially if they have a family. Asset protection is nothing more than a shield the law provides which says, "When you're going to do business, use this, protect yourself, and as long as you're doing it legally, we are going to allow it to stand."

Tax reduction is another break—another legality—given by the IRS and the government which states that if you're incorporated, you're allowed to spend a certain limited amount money for getting health insurance, life insurance, fixing the car, and various other expenses before you pay taxes. For example, if you are self-employed, your taxes—your social security taxes—are about 15.2 percent of what you make. As a corporation you're only paying 7.5 percent and that is a legal tax reduction. A lot of people like to use Nevada and offshore; we use them legally—we do not recommend not paying taxes and we don't advocate avoiding taxes—we reduce taxes legally.

And the final one is the corporate credit that you mentioned. When you individually obtain a line of credit or a loan from a bank, they're going to look at your debt ratio. If you're above the 49 percent mark they're not going to give you a loan. With a corporation you can have 100 percent debt and they can still give you a loan, if you're set up properly and you can show the proper paperwork—the balance sheet, etc. Corporate credit is what allows somebody to have a multi-million dollar company as opposed to an individual who's only going to be able to grow as much as his or her personal credit will allow. So that's the essence of those three.

Wright

You also mentioned offshore, isn't that illegal or unsafe?

Monsour

It's a myth that offshore accounts are illegal or unsafe. Individual accounts are unsafe in the sense that the government—any government—can attach them. Any government can find out who you are; it's just a matter of paper tracing especially now with the Internet. I could put in your Social Security and find out everything about you. Whereas, you can put as much money as you want offshore and then, if it's legal, we'll show you how you pay taxes on that, and do it anonymously. When you're ready to bring it in and the government attempts to collect taxes on it, you can show where you declared it and where you paid the taxes. It is illegal to take money and put it offshore to avoid paying taxes. Again, we're not truly avoiding taxes, we're simply protecting it—we're taking a legitimate business, which we want to grow, and we're protecting it against frivolous lawsuits. Approximately $163 million were paid out in frivolous lawsuits a couple of years ago, so this is what we're looking to provide protection against. It's not illegal—that's a myth.

Wright

Can clients get into trouble by protecting their assets or reducing their taxes?

Monsour

Actually no, it's encouraged. There are Supreme Court decisions supporting that. Congress has, on numerous occasions, discussed that. The IRS specifically has means of helping you reduce your taxes because they are interested in turning the economy around. The more it turns, the more money you make and the more taxes you pay them.

People are willing to help give employment to others when they know their liability is going to be reduced, as long as they're running a legitimate business. By setting up a corporation you can use all these advantages in order to take that commerce forward. So, reducing taxes is perfectly legal.

Once you get onto the state levels there are different rules and regulations that are just incredibly heavy on a business owner. For example, California is the worst; they charge you for just about anything. If the legislature ever woke up and realized how to properly do it, they could bring in ten times the money and have a better working environment. I sent out a proposal to them, but apparently they are not interested.

Wright

On your Web site I noticed that you do a lot of explaining and educating. Aren't you afraid of people going out and doing this on their own?

Monsour

Well, actually, we've had a lot of complaints from our competitors about that. They've said, "You are ruining the business—you're telling everybody the secrets." I'm not telling anybody any secrets; I'm telling them how it is. Filing a paper is not a secret, it's just that people don't want to have to go and read nine years or twenty years worth of information like I have done in order to learn all this stuff. They would just rather have somebody else do it; but when I do it for them and they have that piece of paper, they need to know what to do with it as opposed to just hanging it up on a wall and looking at it. Remember, our slogan is, "The small business development company." How am I going to help you develop if I keep you in the dark? If I don't feed you that information you're never going to grow. As soon as you have that information and know how to use it you're set to go.

Now out of a hundred people I might teach this to, eighty-five may come to me and the other fifteen may decide to do it on their own. By all means, you have at it if you are capable; and if you have the time and are willing to do that. What we found out, however, is that those eighty-five are much more successful than the other fifteen because they don't have to do the testing and see what's going to work and what's not going to work. Of the fifteen about one-half return and we start all over. So we're not afraid of it—we enjoy doing that. Our purpose is to educate; by educating we're going to achieve our goals. If you can do it on your own then God speed.

Wright

Couldn't an attorney or an accountant advise these clients the same as you can?

Monsour

You would think so. You would think, "I need tax reduction, let's go to an accountant," or, "I need to incorporate," or you might want asset protection and you'd go to an attorney. What I have found is about 90 percent of my clients (if not 98 percent) come to me saying, "Oh, my accountant says not to set up a corporation," or, "My attorney says that's not a good idea." When I ask why, they'll reply, "Well, I'm not quite sure." When I ask what kind of attorney they have hired, I find that they either have a criminal defense attorney they've known in the past or an immigration attorney or the attorney specializes in some other field. This is a specialty—you don't go to a criminal defense attorney if you're having an immigration issue or vice versa and it amazes me that accountants will say no to incorporation because, (1) it is a benefit to the client and (2) it's going to generate more business for the accountant.

When I do the paperwork and you're set to go, you don't need to come back to me, but the accountant expects a lot of repeat business—at least once a year. We offer year-round consulting to our clients; but most attorneys and most accountants seem to see themselves as experts because of their title. They're not experts because they don't have experience in this area and they're not giving out the right information for the most part.

Wright

You know, I've had trouble in the past—in the immediate past—understanding the difference. I've always incorporated businesses but now people are choosing to form Limited Liability Companies (LLC). I read the papers and they look the same as a corporation to me.

Monsour

Well that's because they're a hybrid. They're a mixture of a partnership and a corporation. I like LLCs for certain things. If you and I are going into a joint venture, instead of signing a partnership—which is going to still keep us individually liable in case something happened—I would set up an LLC. What that does is allow all of our taxes to be handled as a partnership but all of our business activity will be under a corporation, thus protecting our personal assets. It's the best of both worlds in that sense.

What I have found is that some banks and institutions don't want to deal with LLCs as opposed to a corporation—either a "C" or an "S" corporation—for the credit side of things. Don't forget, LLCs are a relatively new thing; they are only about twenty or thirty years old, so a lot of bankers aren't quite as familiar with them. A lot of clients want it because it sounds good—it's the latest wave. The way we usually set it up is, for example, you decide to be a real estate investor and you buy an apartment building. We'll set up a separate LLC, with an address at, say, 123 Pine Street (usually wherever the property is located). The only person involved with the business is you, but if a tenant slips and falls, they're only allowed to sue the LLC. They will only be able to collect from the LLC and you will have protected your personal assets from that lawsuit.

Wright

What about the many companies out there that do incorporation services or credit work; are they any good?

Monsour

There are some very good ones. It would be a lie for me to say no; there are some great ones out there. However, as I said earlier, there's no one company or person that does everything under one roof.

There are some that are really horrendous. There is one company I heard about that has been sued nineteen to twenty times because of the scams they're running. We keep servicing and trying to remedy their former clients' situations. They will incorporate you no matter what you want to do and they'll give you partial truths—they don't have to lie to you but they don't give you the full sentence. For example, they tell their clients, "You can incorporate in California and only pay a $100 a year to incorporate." Well that's not true because starting with your second year you have to pay a minimum of $800 in taxes. They somehow neglect to address that and when confronted with it they deny the taxes will be due. Or they'll tell you, "Incorporate in Nevada and avoid taxes." Well, you're only avoiding state taxes but if you live in a particular state like California and California finds out about it, they're still going to want their taxes from that money earned. There are a lot of companies, yes, and there are some that are even cheaper than we are, but many are incorporating companies we are not.

We are a Business Development Company. We walk you through every step, we find out what you want to do, and we configure a plan specifically for you. Cookie cutter plans rarely work and we are not dealing with the cookie cutter system. Cookie cutters do not educate and support—we do. You can go through most of these companies online, if not all of them, and you can get a corporation for a fraction of what we charge, and we don't charge that much either, but all they're doing is pushing paper—you want a corporation? What do you want to call it? ABC Inc.? Here you go, you give them the check and they'll give you the paperwork and go take care of it on your own. Whereas we not only do that part but we also tell you that if you have any questions let us know, and by the way, make sure you do this, this, this, and this. We have twenty-three different services we offer—a combination of corporations, credit, asset protection, and legal tax savings. We educate the client. We walk you through the entire process; this way you're getting not only what the other companies are offering but you're saving yourself all of the consulting costs and headaches you are going to have by trying to figure out what to do with this paper now that you have it.

Wright

How do you decide on the type of setup or plan each of your clients need?

Monsour

Again, it's going to vary. Even if I had ten different clients in real estate it's going to vary for each of them if they are going to need the same setup or even a similar setup. I have some clients who want to flip properties—they want to buy it and sell it. They're not going to need the same kind of setup as somebody who's going to buy and hold the property because the one who's going to hold it is going to be subject to potential liability further down the line because he or she is holding the property.

We create plans on an individual basis because we're individuals— every business is unique. Again, it goes back to the education we give and it goes back to that one-year, two-year, five-year, and ten-year plan. I've had people who want to set up corporations and in about five to ten years take it public. I've had other people who are just going into a venture that will last two to three years and then they're going to dissolve the company. The intent, how much money should be spent, and what kind of package is required are going to vary. That's why we decide on the type of setup, which will be different for each client.

Wright

You protect your clients from creditors and sometimes the government. Isn't that a bit risky or scary, not to mention illegal?

Monsour

Again, the government allows us a lot of breaks; it's just that most people aren't educated about them. This relates to a lot of your questions because the accountants and attorneys who should be knowledgeable about this stuff are giving the wrong advice. They do not specialize in that arena. The public has a misconception about the legality of reducing taxes. Information from the government about tax breaks is out there and is available to the public—anybody could look it up.

I am not going to set you up in a corporation so that you can apply for a million dollar credit card from Bank of America, let's say, cash it out, and then skip town. That's not what we're here for and the law doesn't protect you from that kind of activity. What you're protected from is losing personal assets if there is a problem with your business. What we are trying to do is even out the playing field. We're trying to take the frivolous lawsuits that are being thrown at these poor people who are out there working their butt off. These frivolous lawsuits are a misuse of the law; we're taking the law and rebuilding it as it was intended to be—a shield and a legitimate structure with which to run our system.

Wright

What about all the extra paperwork and expense required to set this up?

Monsour

That's where we come in. You need a corporation? All you have to do is fill out a two-sheet application which tells us what you want to call the company and other details, then sign an agreement which says we're not helping you defraud anybody. Aside from that, whether you're running the business as a corporation or as a sole proprietor, you need to maintain your receipts because you need to put those on the tax forms when you fill out your taxes at the end of the year. Instead of putting your business finances with your personal finances, you're keeping your business finances separate. The paperwork is nothing out of the ordinary and it's not cumbersome. It's the exact same paperwork you're going to be receiving regardless of how you run your business; but we have taken care of setting up the paperwork for you ahead of time so that if you are sued, God forbid, or when you pay your taxes, you will be taking advantage of the tax breaks the government allows. It may cost you an extra $500 or $1000 for an accountant to do two separate tax returns—one for you and one for your business—but when you look at the savings it's enormous. You know that $1000 becomes pennies on the dollar in savings.

Wright

What about a trust? Wouldn't a trust protect my assets in addition to reducing my taxes?

Monsour

No, and here's why: The reason I don't like trusts—one of the biggest reasons—is they're too complicated for most people, including attorneys, to use. The requirements and duties of the trustee—the person in charge of the trust—and his or her obligations in running it are burdensome compared to being CEO of a corporation. Nobody should ever want to be a trustee. If you make a slight mistake, even if it's a reasonable one, you can still be held personally liable. And most trusts reach their maximum tax bracket when they reach $7000 or $9000 in income, which is totally the opposite of what we're trying to do with a corporation and trying to legally reduce taxes.

The only trust I do recommend is a trust to make sure that when you die you are passing on everything to your family or whomever you want without a will. You can make that private so it's more of a post-death thing—it's more of a decedent issue.

As far as living and protecting your assets and reducing your taxes with a trust, that is a misconception. There are a few out there because there are a variety of trusts but very few people can set them up correctly and very few people can even learn how to manage them properly. As far as being sued, a corporation can protect you best. A corporation is very, very straightforward, whereas a trust is not; that's why we don't recommend them.

Wright

Your prices seem extremely reasonable, if not low, for all the services that you offer. Is there a reason?

Monsour

Yes. The two main people in my business include a gentleman named Erik Salmon and myself. Erik handles the credit aspect of the business; I had been doing this before I met him. When he came on board we sat down together and discussed what our stumbling blocks were. We made a list of all the pros and all the cons. Obviously we wanted to keep all the pros. We came up with a solution for each one of the cons; the biggest one was the pricing.

For example, you want to set up a corporation, your corporate credit profile, and you want consulting year-round. Any question you have you can e-mail to us; we will get you an answer in twenty-four to forty-eight hours, depending on how complex the problem is. If you have an emergency you can call us on the phone. Our price for that is $2,700–$3,900, which is cheaper than the average cost of having an attorney set up one corporation for you.

That's another thing we've been having problems with. Our competitors say we are undercutting the market. Our goal is to help people succeed not to bleed them of their seed money. So if you're coming out to start your business and you're just leaving a $30,000 to $40,000 a year job, you don't have $10,000 to $20,000 to start your business. By setting it up for $2,000 we're helping you to succeed. This enables us to stay true to our motto. Everything we do relates to our motto which is to help you succeed. I can't help you succeed if I'm bleeding you of your startup money.

Wright

If I elected to have you do corporate work for me with several businesses I own, would you come to me or do I have to send things to you?

Monsour

Well, right now I'm in California. If you were in New York, for example, we would handle a lot of logistics on the phone. Once we were ready to get things going I would then fly out to your location. We would sit down and handle things. I have clients in Florida, Texas, Chicago, Washington, and Australia. We do business around the world and we like to go to our client if necessary. Not everyone requires it. Why? Because sometimes we need a lot of files if you are already in business but you're not yet incorporated. It is not reasonable to have you haul your entire office to ours. We like to go to the client whenever necessary.

That's one of the things we're trying to do now—we're trying to look for quality, honest, and ethical people to be able to provide these services to clients in their areas so that the few people we have aren't having to travel across the country. We want our clients to be comfortable. They know their surroundings, they can answer the questions, and they're not edgy. If I ask a question and you're at my office and the answer is in your drawer in your office across the country, we'd have a problem. So, going to the client's place of business is much more efficient.

Wright

As I understand it, you are a consultant; do you also give legal or accounting advice?

Monsour

No we do not. It sounds like a lot of what we're doing is legal work and accounting but there is a fine line between business and legal and accounting. What we're doing is saying this is what you can do.

With every document we give out there's a statement at the bottom that says we do not give legal or tax advice, that you should consult a knowledgeable attorney or accountant. You need someone who knows about this particular type of setup because remember, 98 percent of accountants and attorneys have no clue. Even though I went through law school and received my J.D., I don't claim to give legal advice because: (1) I cannot and (2) I do not want to do that because if you have an attorney I don't want to infringe on that relationship.

What we try to do is develop your business as a benefit of incorporating. We explain the benefits for which you are eligible. If you have any specific legal or specific tax issue that you need handled, you need to go to your attorney or accountant. If you don't have one we have people to whom we can refer you.

Wright

I've heard that you don't reveal any client's name or use any client testimonials. Why is that?

Monsour

Clients come to me and want to protect their assets. A lot of people who want to protect their assets want to keep it private. You don't want to be standing on the street corner saying, "Hey, I have ten million dollars in a bank account. Come sue me!"

When we set up businesses we set up an organization that does business with the public. It's the organization that could possibly be sued. It's what I like to call the "disposable corporation." Then we set one up that protects your identity from the public. It's a private company—nobody knows you own it and that's where we are going to put your assets. Given all of that it would be ridiculous of me to say, "Hey, we have David here who set up a corporation and he's going to tell you how good we are, how well we worked for him, and how well we protected him. He's worth millions and he's going to show you how and why you should use us so that you can be set up like he is." You came to us for privacy, not for publicity.

This has been the biggest hindrance we've had. People want references and are asking us, "Well, I need to talk to somebody—I need to speak to some of your former clients." I do have some clients who are willing to give me testimonials. They allow me to use their initials only, which is fine, but we're still hesitant to do even that. We might start doing that because some of our clients say they are willing to do it to help us. We might actually start putting some of those on our Web site.

Our web site is undergoing some updating right now because of legalities that are taking place and we might use testimonials, but we will keep it as private as possible because that's our goal. Our goal is to help you succeed and for you not have to pay out any money to defend yourself against a lawsuit just because somebody knows you have money.

Sam Walton was worth billions and yet drove around a pickup truck that was thirty years old. Some people enjoy that and who am I to say that he should be driving a Rolls Royce?

Wright

Well, what a great conversation. Today we've been talking with Louis Monsour, who is the President and Chief Executive Officer of IBS Enterprises, Inc. He has extensive experience in real estate investment, as a consultant, and in the entertainment industry. And I think we have found out here that he knows a whole lot about what he's talking about. Listen to him on www.KTSA.com.

Louis, thank you so much for being with us today on *Pillars of Success*.

Monsour

Thank you, it was my pleasure.

About The Author

LOUIS MONSOUR is the President and Chief Executive Officer of IBS Enterprises, Inc. He has nine years of experience in asset protection, legal tax reduction, corporate credit and finance, and overall business consulting. Mr. Monsour strives at educating the entrepreneur and current business owner in the areas of asset protection, legal tax savings, establishing proper corporate credit, and taking on business ventures, which include real estate, international trade, and the entertainment industry. Mr. Monsour has extensive experience in law, real estate, and as an investor and consultant. He also has experience in the entertainment industry.

Although he is a law school graduate he does not practice law. He enjoys consulting and has clients from various industries such as entertainment, real estate investment, contractors, and high tech companies. In addition to running the business and his many involvements with various industries, Mr. Monsour was a professor at Westwood College where he taught business ethics, criminal law, and criminal procedure among other subjects. Currently he is the host of the *Make It and Keep It* hour on KTSA 550AM or www.KTSA.com on Saturdays from 1:00–2:00 PM. He is married with three boys of ten, eight, and two years of age.

Louis Monsour

IBS Enterprises, Inc.

Phone: 626.737.1477

E-mail: Lmonsour@IBSEnterprises.com

Chapter Four

KIMBERLY ALYN

THE INTERVIEW

David E. Wright (Wright)

We're talking with Kimberly Alyn today. Kim is an author and professional keynote speaker. Kim has overcome insurmountable odds in her life to become a successful entrepreneur. She is a no-nonsense, sarcastic, humorous, and motivational speaker. Her stories and presentations have entertained, inspired, educated, motivated, and sometimes irritated people around the globe.

Kim "tells it like it is" and her open, honest, and upfront approach calls people into accountability for the level of success in their own lives. Kim wholeheartedly believes in living life to the fullest with passion and purpose. She often says, "If you're not living on the edge, you're taking up too much dang room!"

Kimberly Alyn, welcome to *Pillars of Success*.

Kimberly Alyn (Alyn)

Thank you David, it's my pleasure! Besides, it's raining in California today, so I can't go outdoors anyway—

Wright

Well, lucky for us!

Kimberly, there are many definitions for success. How would *you* define success?

Alyn

You're right, there are so many definitions for success. I have heard numerous speakers and authors define success differently. I do believe success is defined differently for every person. If I asked you what defines success, your answer would be different from mine and my answer would be different from another's.

I define success like this: "Using your God-given gifts and talents to fulfill your God-given purpose in life." It's that simple. We all have different talents and gifts. If we are using those to the very best of our ability to accomplish what we were put on this earth for, then we're successful. If we allow those talents and gifts to be wasted or go un-used, then we are failures. Average people fulfill their dreams, but successful people fulfill their purpose.

Success is not measured by money. I have seen plenty of wealthy people who squander their talents, their gifts, and their lives. I have seen plenty of failures who have money! I have also seen plenty of successful people who earn a moderate income. They have a definitive purpose in life, they know what it is, and they use their talents and gifts to fulfill that purpose. They are happy, content, and productive. The money usually follows. Now *that's* success!

Now, I have also heard it said, "If at first you don't succeed, then skydiving is not for you" but that's another story for another time—

Wright

That's funny! Kim, what do you think is one of the biggest obstacles to becoming successful?

Alyn

The inability to overcome adversity is one of the biggest obstacles to becoming successful. The road to contentment, happiness, and success is paved with obstacles far too great for some people to overcome. For others, those very obstacles serve to strengthen them and mold them into great success stories. For some, the challenges of life cause a driving force within them that takes them to heights not recommended for the faint of heart.

Horace once said, "Adversity has the effect of eliciting talents, which in prosperous circumstances would have lain dormant." Some people don't allow adversity to do just that. Instead, they wallow in the circumstances that surround them and fail to use them to grow and learn.

People will inevitably experience setbacks and failures in life, and the response to that adversity will determine the level of success that can be reached. We all choose how we will respond to adversity. We can respond like an ice cube, a grape, or a Joshua tree. When all three of these are faced with the same scorching desert heat of adversity, they all respond differently. The ice cube starts out solid and unrelenting, but after facing the heat of adversity, ends up weakened and melted. The grape starts out soft and tender, but under the heat of adversity, ends up shriveled and unrecognizable. But the Joshua tree flourishes in the scorching desert heat and the hotter the sun, the more it thrives. In fact, without the heat of adversity, it would die.

Adversity can either strengthen us, or it can weaken us. If we choose to let it strengthen us, we can sharpen our talents and be more successful in life. If we would all learn to live like a Joshua tree, we would flourish under adversity!

Wright

You sound like someone speaking from experience. What are some obstacles you have had to overcome to be successful?

Alyn

Wow, how long is this book? This could take awhile! My life has been filled with obstacles beginning at birth. My mother left me when I was two months old and never came back. I was sent to an orphanage for six months until my father was released from jail and could take custody of me. He married a woman eleven years older than he was and left me with her.

We lived in extreme poverty and I found myself without any parental supervision most of the time. I didn't find out she wasn't my real mother until I was ten years old. I lived with my father from the time I was ten until I was almost fifteen years old. He moved me up to the hills in Santa Cruz, California, where he grew more than 200 pot (marijuana) plants! We had no electricity, no running water, and no indoor plumbing. My father was a drug dealer, car thief, and fake I.D. manufacturer. This is a man who thought reality was a crutch for people who couldn't handle drugs! He was lazy, smoked a lot of pot, and would make comments like, "Kimberly, ambition is just a poor excuse for not having enough sense to be lazy."

He was arrested when I was eleven and we were placed on the witness protection program in lieu of him serving twenty years in prison. I had to change schools six times and my last name four times, all within two years.

My father was mean, abusive, and violent. He broke my arm when I was ten years old and often lashed out in fits of anger. When I was fourteen, his girlfriend was living with us and she was only sixteen years old. I rebelled against everything he stood for. He finally kicked me out of the house when I was almost fifteen. I lived with different people while I finished high school. Education was not a high priority in my family, and no one had graduated high school, much less even considered college.

By the grace of God I knew I had a purpose, and I knew it wasn't to live in failure. I couldn't afford to go to college, so I studied at the local library. I read every book I could get my hands on about leadership, success, communication skills, and overcoming adversity. I began to study what successful people did with their lives, their time, and their talents.

I started to evaluate what my gifts and talents were. I owned my first business when I was nineteen years old—I was a clown for children's birthday parties! Later I owned a photography business and then went on to open my own financial planning firm (where I became the fastest woman in history to obtain my financial certifications, which are the equivalent to a four-year degree). I went back to college and received my bachelor's degree in management and my master's in organizational management.

I have also made a lot of bad choices in my life that have caused me and others undue adversity. Sometimes the obstacles we face are not caused by others or circumstances; they are caused by us! I had to face a lot of issues within myself and make a lot of changes to become the person I was created to be. I had to learn to make better choices and try and make amends for the bad choices that were made.

I have always tried to let the adversities in my life strengthen me and not weaken me. I have always believed that God had a very definitive purpose for my life and even when I got off track, He would get me back on track. He gave me talents and gifts that would help me fulfill my purpose regardless of my trials, tribulations, circumstances, and poor choices.

Wright

What a story! Do you find that people find it more difficult to make excuses for failure when they hear you speak?

Alyn

Absolutely! I speak a lot about perseverance, excellence, accountability, and success. Before people know my history—and believe me, I have only hit the tip of the iceberg here—they usually say, "Yeah Kim, but you don't understand. I grew up in poverty. I lived in an abusive home. I didn't have an opportunity to succeed. I've made some stupid mistakes." When they hear that I once lived on a bag of pancake mix and fresh-picked berries for two weeks when I was only thirteen years old, they stop with the excuses. People are always shocked to hear about my background and what I came through. I try to explain to people that we are capable of overcoming any and all obstacles in life and that I speak from personal experience, not lofty theory.

Unfortunately, most people would rather use their circumstances and their past as an excuse to fail, because there's too much accountability in success. You have to come to grips with the fact that your life has a purpose. You have to take ownership for your life and the dumb mistakes you have made. You have to put your talents and skills to work instead of allowing them to be wasted. It's much easier to sit around and whine about how bad your life is, how bad your job is, how bad society is, and why you just can't get a break! Success means you have to quit complaining, get off your butt, and do something about it! As Charles Swindoll once said, "Only 10 percent of life is what happens to you; the other 90 percent is how you choose to respond to it."

Wright

Fear seems to be a major factor for people. They fear failure or maybe even success. What role has fear played in your life?

Alyn

What a great question! First of all, I believe the words of Mark Twain wholeheartedly when he said, "Unless a creature be part coward, it is not a compliment to say it is brave." I had my demons of fear, and I had to overcome those fears to become successful.

I was terrified of public speaking. The first time I ever spoke in front of a group I was fourteen years old. It was disastrous and I swore I would never speak in front of people again! I was able to dodge that bullet for many years. Then I realized that the fear was controlling my life. I read a quote by Dale Carnegie that said, "If you want to overcome fear, do that which you fear and keep on doing it until you have a record of successful experiences behind you."

As I became determined to overcome this fear, I developed a skill and a talent that I never thought possible. If someone would have told me at the age of fourteen I would one day be a professional speaker, I would have laughed in their face (or thrown up in fear!).

I was also extremely afraid of small planes and heights. I wanted to conquer these fears as well. It took me nine months and a tremendous amount of sweat, tears, and exhaustion, but I conquered those fears. On December 3, 1996, I became a licensed pilot! Overcoming that fear and getting my pilot's license was one of the hardest things I have ever done in my life.

It didn't help matters that my local airport where I was learning to fly had a mean air traffic controller. I was practicing my landings one day and I bounced that little Cessna 152 all the way down the runway. Within seconds his voice came over the radio, "Um, did you just land, or were you shot down?"

I gave it right back to him: "Look buddy, that wasn't my fault, and I know it wasn't your fault—it must have been the asphalt!"

It took a tremendous amount of commitment and perseverance to see that goal through. There were times when I didn't think I could do it. When I first started with an instructor, I would have little panic attacks when we got in the air. I tried to hide it as much as possible, but it overwhelmed me at times. I didn't tell anyone I was getting my pilot's license—I wanted it to be a surprise. Besides, if I failed, then no one would ever know I even tried! At least that was my reasoning at the time.

I'm glad I stretched myself and did it. I was tired of letting fear rule my life. Now I laugh in the face of fear as I fly over the LAX airport in California. When you learn to face your fears and overcome them, you begin to reach new heights in life! I believe this so strongly, that the first book I ever wrote is on the very subject (*SOAR*).

Wright

Most people would just try to get on an airplane and fly more often to conquer that fear. You don't do anything small, do you?

Alyn

No, I'm with Helen Keller who said, "Life is either a daring adventure, or nothing at all." Go big, or go home! I've just gotten to the point in my life where I just don't want to settle for mediocrity. I've done that in the past, and it didn't work out very well for me. God created us for so much more, and it just doesn't make sense to settle for anything less.

We were all given the tools and talents we need to succeed. We don't always discover that early on in life (and some people never discover that at all!). The great news is it's never too late to start again. It's never too late to explore our gifts and talents and begin to put them to good use. It's never too late to start fulfilling our purpose in life. It's never too late to start making the right choices instead of the wrong ones. Every day we have a blank slate, and every day we each decide what gets written in our book of life. Each day I attempt to make my life better than it was yesterday. I try to treat people better, be a kinder person, make use of my life in a better way, and leave a positive impact on the people I encounter in my life.

Wright

You've had an amazing life Kim. Do you get the opportunity to share your life stories with a lot of people to help them overcome their obstacles and succeed?

Alyn

I have been blessed with the opportunity to speak to many different groups on many different topics. Life has taught me so many valuable lessons that my stories come out in every topic. I have the opportunity to talk to women's groups, corporations, municipalities, youth groups, churches, and just about anyone who will listen! I think my dogs are tired of hearing my stories!

A few years ago I had the opportunity to speak to a junior high class of high-risk kids. These kids were considered most at risk for dropping out of school, doing drugs, or committing crimes. They all came from broken homes. Maybe one parent was a drug user, maybe a parent was in prison, or both parents never graduated high school, or they had no parents in their lives at all. Some of the kids were in foster care after being terribly abused. Some had already spent time in juvenile hall. All of them believed they didn't have a chance in life.

I think they were all surprised to hear that I had experienced nearly everything they had experienced, and I still overcame. I tried to communicate some important concepts for them such as: If we look around and dwell on our circumstances or our past, it's easy to believe we'll ever rise above it all. We are defined not by our circumstances, but by our response to trial and tribulation. And while we can not always control the outer world, we can control the drive, the strength, and the will of our inner self and no person, event, or crisis can ever steal that away—it can only be surrendered. Within each and every one of us is an aspiring greatness longing to be free. The only obstacle preventing that freedom is surrendering to life's circumstances.

I believe we can all rise above the circumstances that surround us and use the obstacles and challenges in our lives to become stronger and more compassionate people. I believe we can all overcome the adversity in our lives to fulfill our purpose. I know it's possible, because I have had to do just that in my own life.

I was amazed at how these kids responded. Many came up to me afterwards and confided in me that they had lost hope. After seeing someone who was actually able to overcome severe obstacles in life, these kids left with a renewed hope for the future. I left with a renewed passion for my purpose—my story had made a difference in someone's life.

We all have stories to tell. Some of our stories serve as a warning to others. (God knows I have plenty of those!) Some serve as an encouragement and inspiration to others. There's purpose in everything that happens to us and everything we do. We need to spend more of our lives in a mode of purposefulness and not so much on autopilot. Without purpose, we will wander aimlessly through life continuing to strive for success and never obtaining it. Success comes to those who fashion their lives around the purpose they were created for and pursue that purpose with passion.

Wright

You mentioned passion. How important do you think passion is for the average person when it comes to success?

Alyn

Passion and purpose are paramount to success. One person with passion will accomplish more than one hundred who are mildly motivated. You must have passion for what you do in life. I have asked people to think about this: What would you do with your life if you didn't have to work? Where would you spend your time and energy? Once you answer that question, you may know where your passion lies. Now, try to find a way to earn a living doing just that (of course this assumes your passion is legal!). I also encourage people to at least find *something* they are passionate about and spend time doing that even if it can't be their fulltime job. Having said that, I do believe if there is a strong enough will there is a clear enough way.

I have never met a successful person who did not have passion and purpose. I look at someone like Walt Disney. Here's a man who, as child got behind in school by two grade levels. Now most people would consider someone like him well on their way to failure. Instead, his teacher encouraged him to do what he loved: drawing cartoons and acting. So Walt started taking classes at an art institute on the weekends. He helped his dad with a paper route to pay for the classes.

Walt Disney never made it past his freshman year in high school, but his passion and purpose took him further than anyone ever imagined. He endured so many failures and obstacles along the way, but he believed, "If you can dream it, you can do it." And that's exactly what he did. He pursued his passion and he fulfilled his purpose. I wonder what would have happened to Walt had he not had a teacher with the wisdom to encourage him to follow his passion. Sometimes we don't have anyone to encourage us, and we have to drive ourselves toward that passion. Either way, that is the surest and easiest way to success: follow your passion and fulfill your purpose.

Wright

Walt Disney is a great example of success. Are there other people who have influenced your life and your view of success?

Alyn

Yes, there are so many leaders and role models throughout history who have influenced me. There have also been people in my life through the years who have affected my life in so many ways. I know this is going to sound strange for some people, but my father had a huge influential impact on my life and how I defined success. He was a role model—an example of what I did *not* want to become. I saw the things he did and how unsuccessful he was in life and how little purpose he had, and I knew I wanted something different. I watched the choices he made and I didn't make those same choices. I watched the people he associated with and I didn't associate with those types of people. I watched the books he read and I didn't read those books. I think a lot of people miss opportunities to really learn from not just successful people, but unsuccessful people. Watch what they do, and don't do it!

I also feel strongly that we need to model after successful people as well. There are many leaders throughout history whom I admire, respect, and study in an effort to improve myself. If I had to pick the most influential leader, role model example, and my ultimate view of a successful person, I would have to say Jesus Christ. Here's a leader who had passion and purpose. He knew His purpose and He lived His entire life to fulfill that one purpose. That makes Him the most successful leader I have ever known. He spoke with passion and conviction whether people wanted to hear the message or not. And a lot of people miss this, but He also had a sarcastic edge to his speeches at times, and I dig that about Him!

He exemplified love and forgiveness, honesty and integrity, character, strength, humility, and servant hood—all the necessary elements for a successful leader. He was the most influential leader of all time. He's the only leader in history who split time in half (B.C. and A.D.), and today He boasts more followers throughout history than any other leader—ever. That's a pretty good indicator of good leadership, because as the proverb says, "He who thinks he leads but has no followers is only taking a walk."

Wright

You refer to yourself as a "Sarcastic Motivational Speaker." I notice you have a fun edge to your style—is that what you're referring to?

Alyn

I once heard it said that sarcastic humor is like a rubber sword—it allows you to make your point without drawing blood. Yes, I have a very sarcastic side to me, and it inevitably comes out in my speaking and my stories. I try to keep life in perspective with lots of humor. I read a quote once by the most commonly quoted person ever ("Unknown"): "Humor reduces people and problems to their proper proportions." I couldn't agree more. Pretty much anything stressful you're going through can be laughed about six months from now, so why not laugh about it now?

I poke fun at everyone and everything, but mostly myself. There's a lot of material there! I believe humor is a basic essential for success. Henry Ward Beecher once said, "Humor makes all things tolerable." And there is always some element of truth in humor, no matter how small. When was the last time you heard a joke about a father-in-law?

It is a physiological fact that stress and laughter cannot occupy the same space at the same time. You cannot experience the state of stress while you are laughing. It's just not possible. Test it out sometime and see how true it is. The average six-year-old laughs 300 times a day. The average adult laughs only seventeen times a day. Adults subject themselves to more stress and they need more laughter. Kids don't walk around all stressed out—they can't, because they are too busy laughing. You can't be stressed when you're laughing.

Negative states don't just happen to you. In every situation in life you get to choose how you will respond. You may not always be able to control what happens to you, but you can control how you respond to it (unless you have PMS, in which case you're not really in control!). Most people live their lives as if they have no choice in how they respond to conflict, adversity, or stress. They allow negative circumstances to control their lives and the course their lives will take. People tend to choose an attitude that comes naturally instead of consciously choosing an attitude that will do themselves and everyone around them the most good.

Laughter crowds out any negative attitude you have entertained. Laughter creates an instant positive state of mind. If you can find the humor in anything, you can have a positive attitude at your fingertips. Laughter is one of the built-in mechanisms God gave us for staying happy and healthy. "A cheerful heart is good medicine, but a crushed spirit dries up the bones"—Proverbs 17:22. The original Hebrew definition of medicine is "a cure." A cheerful heart can provide a cure to our bodies, but a crushed spirit can lead to deterioration. This fact has been proven medically.

Dr. Lee Berk of Loma Linda University in California has studied the effects of laughter on the immune system. Studies prove that laughter lowers blood pressure, reduces stress hormones, and boosts the immune system. Additionally, laughter triggers the release of endorphins, which are the body's natural painkillers. As a result, laughter creates a sense of well-being. Medical experts now believe that laughter can reduce pain and assist in the healing process. A good belly laugh is considered the equivalent to "an internal jogging." In fact, laughing one hundred times is the equivalent to fifteen minutes on an exercise bike or ten minutes on a rowing machine. So if you needed to lose weight, you could *literally* laugh your butt off!

Well I guess you can tell that I have very strong feelings about the importance of humor. Aristotle said, "Total absence of humor renders life impossible." I agree wholeheartedly!

Wright

I can tell you're big on humor. I think that's great! Kim, are there any secrets to success you would like to close with today?

Alyn

Yes, there is only one secret to success and it's this (drum roll please): Success is no secret! Throughout history, people who have been successful have been doing the same thing! I have yet to see anyone come out of the secret success closet saying, "I lived my life for myself. I slept in, watched television and drank beer all day. I was lazy, dishonest, apathetic, and without vision. And you know what? Success just fell in my lap!" I'm not a big gambler, but I would bet your life savings you're probably never going to hear that!

The obvious principals of success haven't changed one bit since the beginning of time: Know your purpose. Have some passion. Do the right thing. Take ownership for your actions. Get off your butt! Be accountable. Be dependable. Persevere until you succeed. Grow from adversity. Keep things in perspective. Tell the truth. Stop making excuses and start taking action. Say you're sorry when you've hurt someone else. Forgive and move on. Fix your mistakes. Have a sense of humor. Don't act like the world owes you something. Learn from your failures. Pay your dues. Work hard. Improve yourself daily. Educate yourself (the library is free). Exercise common sense. Be adaptable.

It's just not brain surgery. It's not rocket science. It's not that difficult. Study what successful people do and do that. Study what unsuccessful people do and don't do that.

About The Author

KIMBERLY ALYN is a professional keynote speaker and author. She provides self-improvement tips with laughter and sarcasm. Her hilarious stories and "tell it like it is" approach are over the top and people love it!

Kim tackles topics that every person and every business can relate to—topics that everyone thinks about but few ever talk about. The universal principals of successful living are seen in a whole new light when Kim takes the stage! Her popular keynote address is taken from her latest book project (due for release in 2006) *It's Not Brain Surgery—Simple Tips to Getting a Grip on a More Successful Life.*

Writing is one of Kim's passions. She is author of: *How to Deal With Annoying People* (with Bob Phillips, PhD), *101 Leadership Reminders, Public Speaking is Not for Wimps, Soar,* and *My Favorite Sarcastic Sayings.*

In her spare time, Kim enjoys flying, motorcycle riding, drawing, and writing. Kim also likes to spend time with family and friends engaging in outdoor activities. Kim believes in living life to the fullest and having some stinkin' fun in life!

Kimberly Alyn

1115 Toro Street Suite G

San Luis Obispo, CA 93401

Phone: 800.821.8116

E-mail: Kim@KimberlyAlyn.com

www.KimberlyAlyn.com

Chapter Five

STEVE DOUGLAS

THE INTERVIEW

David E. Wright (Wright)

Today we're talking with Steve Douglas. Steve brings more than thirty years of professional sales experience that involves three different industries. His clients have included professional athletes, universities, major corporations, manufacturers, and entrepreneurs alike. Steve has spoken to such groups as State Farm Insurance Companies, The Insurance and Financial Advisors Association for the State of Alaska, The National Association of Property Managers, and many athletic sports events for The University of Florida.

Steve, welcome to *Pillars of Success!*

Steve Douglas (Douglas)

Thanks Dave!

Wright

So, how do you define success?

Douglas

Dave, I've heard so many times before that success is the continuous realization of worthwhile goals; but personally, I think there's far more to it than this. Real success must be identified and continuously connected with your true, unique and authentic purpose. In other words, why are you here? Why did you choose your life's work? What is your central and foundational purpose in relationships, from your family and friends to clients and prospects, all the way to meeting a stranger on the street?

The great Scot, William Wallace, centuries ago said it best in regards to purpose, "Every man dies, not every man really lives." The word of emphasis is "really." That word should be highlighted in yellow, circled in red, underlined and stars and asterisks should be placed all around it. For those who don't recognize the name, William Wallace, Mel Gibson portrayed him in the 1995 movie *Braveheart*.

William Wallace not only knew his unique and authentic purpose but he lived for his purpose and died for his purpose. I believe everyone has a unique and authentic purpose, but so many don't know what it is because it has been buried for so long within the distractions of everyday life. The central message in my presentation of how to create a boomerang of blessings in your life is all about finding, experiencing, and truly living the *"really."* I share with others not only why it is so essential to live a life of purpose, but I also share with others how to uncover their purpose. From my own personal experience all I can say is, when you uncover your purpose in life and you give it freely to the needs of the world, you'd better fasten your seatbelt because your life is about to be radically transformed...for the better!

The first fifty years of my life I didn't know my true purpose; but I was fortunate and blessed in that I still experienced a life I considered highly effective and very successful by my own standards. The last four years I've lived with knowing, owning, embracing, and carrying out my life's purpose and the difference is not only astonishing, but at times almost unbelievably overwhelming.

You see David, once you uncover and act out your true purpose, then your life from then on becomes a life that represents nothing short of excellence. The way I describe it is you get into a "zone"—you get into the flow—if you know what I mean. You find your "sweet spot" in the grand scheme of things. You go to higher ground in terms of being connected and fulfilled in life and in all of its experiences. When your unique, God-given talents and abilities are carried out with purpose, and when it intersects with the needs of the world, therein lies your gladness; therein lies your greatest joy; therein lies a life of excellence.

Wright

Since you feel that purpose is so essential to the fulfillment of the quality of life you may or may not live, would you mind sharing with me *your* purpose?

Douglas

Not at all, David, I appreciate you asking. "My purpose is to serve and to inspire, in making a positive and profound difference in the lives of others."

Wright

So what motivates you and how do you keep your motivation full throttle?

Douglas

I'm glad you asked that, David. It's funny you should ask, because this is part of one of the central topics in my seminars. I coined a phrase that relates to your question: "Choose to have your perspiration come from inspiration, and not from motivation, so you can end a life of quiet desperation." In other words, your life's work—your perspiration—is best served if your inspiration is the source for attaining results in your professional and personal life.

Unfortunately, far too many people confuse motivation with inspiration. Where the confusion comes in, and where the false perception takes place, is in their one, and only one, similarity: they both get results. In fact, if you are personally motivated or authentically inspired you can create enormous results either way. The disparity or difference between the two—and that difference is gargantuan—is in the "*way*" the results are derived. It's what I call "experiencing your emotional dance with others and experiencing your emotional dance with life." With our interview, time doesn't permit me to go into as much depth as I do in my presentation. I will tell you this though, the emotional dance of the inspired is far more beautiful, connected, and natural than that of the motivated soul.

Wright

What would you say would be the biggest contribution to your professional success?

Douglas

Being blessed in the early years of my professional career in the realization and utilization of our greatest power, given to us by The Greatest Power—the power to choose. I learned early on that with every choice in life there comes with that choice a consequence that we may or may not like or want. So through the experiences in my life I learned it was paramount to become a master of making excellent choices so that excellent consequences would result. Really, David, when you think about it, it's our choices and the resulting consequences that create the colors and the picture of our individual tapestry of life. It really creates the type of legacy we leave behind.

In my seminars I share with the audience what I call core and foundational choices that we need to be making, not just day to day, but literally, moment by moment in order to generate the kind of awesome consequences that we would like to create for ourselves and for others who cross our paths in this beautiful thing called life.

Wright

So how did you begin speaking and why did you choose your particular title of "How to Create a Boomerang of Blessings in Your Life"?

Douglas

My speaking came about not through personal desire but rather from the curiosity of others. I'm currently in the insurance and financial services industry. One year I had the good fortune of being number one in the state of Florida for assets under management among 925 other sales professionals. That same year I was number twenty-ninth nationally out of approximately 17,000 sales professionals. It just wasn't the numbers I was putting up that caused the curiosity to peak, but also because of the area where my sales were being generated.

The town I do business in is a small, blue collar, low-income community. When I first moved here there was a Wal-Mart in the town, which has since closed, as did two of the largest employers. Needless to say this has been a real challenging business environment compared with more economically vibrant communities within Florida. Because I have been blessed with success in spite of that, curiosity was created. The author, Steven Covey says: "You're either an abundance thinker or a scarcity thinker." I am definitely an abundance thinker. I have always enjoyed sharing with and giving to others. Because of this, my speaking requests and activity kicked into high gear.

It was in Pittsburgh, Pennsylvania, where my speaking role was about to be radically altered. I was asked to come back to the Pittsburgh area and create a new presentation that would span a two-day period and involved seven total hours engaged with the audience. The response I received was nothing short of overwhelming. Now I realize that I was asked to create this, not because of chance, but because I was now ready to share my unique and authentic purpose with the needs of others.

Dave, it's been said before "that the only things you can keep in life are the things you give away." From this thought came the boomerang of blessings concept and ultimate title. What I share passionately with my audience are the important and absolute essential things we must give away. By doing so, we not only enrich the lives of others, but we also enrich ourselves in the process. This enrichment process becomes immeasurably more than we could ever ask for or imagine.

Wright

So what do you think are some of the major obstacles that hold people back? Not only in their professional lives, but also from in personal lives.

Douglas

It's definitely a lack of purpose. Henry David Thoreau's famous quote: "Most men lead lives of quiet desperation", was not addressing people with purpose. He was talking clearly about purposeless lives. But even before this obstacle takes hold, it's the constant and endless pursuit of the right answers. What really should be taking place is the pursuit of the right questions, with an open and willing heart and then become quiet and still and listen to our inner voice that speaks to us through our feelings.

Wright

Do you have a quote that was foundational or pivotal in the early development of your personal and professional life?

Douglas

Absolutely. For years, every morning before I went to work, I would read a famous quote by Calvin Coolidge. "Nothing in the world can take the place of persistence. Talent will not; nothing is more common than unsuccessful men with talent. Genius will not; unrewarded genius is almost a proverb. Education will not; the world is full of educated derelicts. Persistence and determination are omnipotent."

Wright

Was there a memorable event for you that you'd like to share with our readers where the power of persistence paid off for you?

Douglas

Yes, sir. I once had a prospect who ran a large department on campus for a major university. The first day I introduced myself he stated that he would never, ever, under any circumstances buy any product from me, *ever*. Like clockwork, I called on this gentleman every week for nine straight months before I finally broke into the account. Not only did this become one of the most profitable accounts I had, but it also developed into a very genuine and respectful friendship. President Coolidge was right on the money with this truth. My success was not generated from talent, genius, or education but through endless persistence.

Wright

So what is your take on positive affirmations?

Douglas

I certainly believe in the old adage "you are what you think." Because of this I've had my own positive affirmations that I've said to myself thousands of times for years. And you know what David? It really works! My positive affirmation is: "Every day, in every way, by the loving grace of God, I'm becoming stronger, happier, healthier, wealthier, and my life is full of peace and love."

Wright

In the area of sales, with your thirty plus years of experience, how would you describe and what is the distinction between sales professionals who would grade out an "A," "B," or "C" for their occupational performance?

Douglas

David, obviously nothing happens until you're in front of a client or prospect. Once you get in front of them, the separation and great divide takes hold. What I mean by this, is the "C" person, I would describe as being a log. No pro activity, total reactionary, your basic order-taker who creates mediocrity at best.

The "B" person I would describe as being monologue. This type is centered on bells, whistles, and product, product, product. They can make things happen, but it's not exactly a warm fuzzy. The motivation is all about making a dollar. A win/win may happen, but all too often and far too often a win/lose takes place. This type of activity may not be illegal, but many times will fall way short of being honorable, ethical, and professional.

The "A" person, on the other hand, is what this hungry world is crying for. I would call the "A" person a master of dialogue. They show they genuinely care about others and they honor them repeatedly by asking value-driven questions and listening intently and then, and only then, do they offer solutions if they are available to needs that have been uncovered in the course of dialogue. What's so spectacular, David, about this process is that it takes all the pressure off of both parties. It's the essence of a win/win, or it's no deal. Here the driver is not about making a dollar, but making a difference. The irony here is that the "A's" will invariably make more dollars than the "B's" due to the fact that they provide far greater value and service to the needs of their clients and prospects. I've also observed, over the years, that the "A's" do not look at work as work. They not only love their work, but they are also incredibly passionate because they realize they are making a significant contribution to others.

Wright

If you had to produce your own personal bumper sticker for your car and the rules were you could never, ever remove it, what do you think yours would say?

Douglas

I normally do not like putting bumper stickers on my car. If I had to, it would definitely be titled, "choose to *really* live."

Wright

A lot of people would stop you on that one, and then you'd have to explain it to them. I'm sure that comes from your love to inspire and to share with others. Steve, I really appreciate you taking all this time with me today to give us this great information. I've learned a lot today.

You are really an exciting and interesting person.

Douglas

Thanks, David, I appreciate it. I hope to see you in Florida sometime.

Wright

Today we've been talking with Steve Douglas. Steve brings years of professional sales experience, as we have seen here today, that involves several industries. He's also spoken to some large corporations and associations. As we have found out today, I think he knows a whole lot about defining success and goal setting and the real importance of purpose in your life.

Steve, thank you so much for being with us today on *Pillars of Success!*

Douglas

Thank you for the opportunity, David.

About The Author

STEVE DOUGLAS brings over thirty years of professional sales experience that involves three different industries. His clients have included professional athletes, universities, major corporations manufacturers, and entrepreneurs alike. Steve has spoken to such groups as State Farm Insurance Companies, The Insurance & Financial Advisors Association for the State of Alaska, The National Association of Property Managers and many athletic support events for the University of Florida.

Steve Douglas

6373 Highway 90

Milton, Florida 32570

Phone: 850.623.0149

www.boomerangofblessings.com

Chapter Six

BETH MARSHALL RAMSAY

THE INTERVIEW

David E. Wright (Wright)
Today we're talking with Beth Marshall Ramsay. She is a business relationship expert and humorist. She is a professional level member of the National Speakers Association.

Beth captivates audiences through her humorous and entertaining style while sharing crucial tips, tools, and information that shares exactly why people do what they do, and what simple things that can be done to understand it, neutralize it, and work with it to dramatically improve relationships instantly.

Beth's most requested workshop is "Working and Playing Well with Others."

Beth is author of *Mean Women Suck: A Survival Guide for Working with Women.*

Beth, welcome to *Pillars of Success.*

Beth Marshall Ramsay (Ramsay)
Thank you David.

Wright
What a great title: *Mean Women Suck!*

Ramsay

This book has a number of interviews with women from different career paths, across a variety of industries and from all levels within companies. They share their experiences, both good and bad, of working with other women.

What motivated me to write *Mean Women Suck* was an extremely hurtful experience that happened to me. I include my story of the ultimate act of deceit and betrayal perpetrated by women I trusted and with whom I worked. What happened was a very well orchestrated smear campaign that was organized by one particular woman I liked and considered a friend. Talk about being blind-sided!

I also include women's opinions on what made their positive working relationships great, and the lessons they learned from the ones that went bad.

Wright

What is the one key principle of success that makes a true achiever?

Ramsay

Power.

Wright

Power? What do you mean by that?

Ramsay

David, I'm not talking about position power—that which comes with a title or a status such as president of the company or CEO—I'm not speaking of that kind of power. And I'm *certainly* not talking about wielding power as a battering ram to run roughshod over others.

What I am referring to is the kind of personal power that comes from a place of confidence, integrity, and intended good will. Personal power is the key to having positive relationships, both in the business world and in our private world.

Wright

So you gain personal power through a better understanding of relationships?

Ramsay

Absolutely! One of the most important skills to possess in the quest for being a true achiever is the ability to successfully interact with other people. Business is based on relationships—good, positive relationships. Successful people understand that a key component is relationship-building with customers, clients, coworkers, management, and subordinates.

In order to maximize success in business (and our personal lives as well) it is critical that we understand how to turn relationships into ones that are more positive, more productive, and more profitable. This is what I call having "relationship savvy."

Wright

I can see where productive and positive relationships would really give personal power. So what are important skills when developing relationships?

Ramsay

Mainly, I see two: one is communication and the other is adaptability. They both can be enhanced by one thing—observation. To be a true achiever in relationship building, observing, and interacting correctly in relationships is vital. We need to develop the skills that are significant to effectively deal with people.

I laugh when I hear the saying, "If it weren't for customers and employees, it'd be great to own your own business!" So, whether we want them to or not, people affect every aspect of doing business! What I'm talking about is being able to develop skills to effectively deal with the difficult people in our lives. We will always have them and as much as we might want to say they don't exist, they do. We should be able to deal more effectively with upset and irate customers, to know what to say to close more sales, to know what it is that a customer is looking for, to boost productivity within the team, and to decrease stress in the workplace.

Wright

Okay, let's take communication first. Don't we all communicate every day?

Ramsay

Of course we do. How many times have we heard that communication is key? It is the key to successful relationships and it is the key to a thriving business with happy customers and a happy staff. But what if it's the wrong communication?

I contend that it is not just communication but the *right* communication that is the key—communicating to others from a deep understanding of what is important to others, what it is that motivates or upsets them, and how we interpret and react to their behaviors. Once we develop a true understanding of typical human behavior—ours first and then those of other people—and we choose to use this understanding effectively, then, and *only* then, will we be using the right communication.

Wright

Do you have some sort of a guideline? I don't want to hold you to setting anything in stone here but is there some sort of a guideline you use to define communication?

Ramsay

There are verbal behaviors and nonverbal behaviors. Listening and hearing key words that are said will provide clues as to what motivates different people, or if they happen to be under a great deal of stress, how they judge others, and what is important to them. This is what I was saying earlier about the powers of observation. The same thing is true for nonverbal communication. We have all heard of the studies showing that most of our communication is nonverbal.

In my workshops and seminars, I share with my audience ways to listen and observe certain things when interacting with someone. It's easy to do by what they say, what they wear, what their office looks like, etc.; you just have to know what to look for. With the knowledge gained in my workshops, participants can apply what they have learned to any relationship and in about a minute or less, accurately decide what kind of people they are communicating with—what is important to that person, understand what motivates that person, recognize what that person's stress behavior is and not get upset or offended by it. Heck, once I share this information, the time saved from coworkers being unproductive because their feelings were hurt is worth the price of my workshop!

Wright

I can certainly believe that! Are you also including body language?

Ramsay

Absolutely. That has something to do with it as well—whether someone is more guarded or more open. For instance, there are some clients who will have a receptionist and I share information with the receptionist about when a customer walks through the door—how the customer approaches her or him can tell her or him a lot of information. There are some people who will come barreling through and some people who are shy and timid. These two kinds of people have a need to be handled differently to be successful in that business relationship.

Wright

Why is the skill—gathering information about these other behaviors—important to know?

Ramsay

When we have a clear understanding of ourselves, which is important, we have to understand ourselves first and then we can better understand what makes us do the things we do. It makes us also better able to understand others with whom we interact on a daily basis and I mean *everybody*. This can mean friends, spouses, those dreaded in-laws, coworkers, bosses, and even our children! We will have a better understanding of how and why these people do what they do. There is a logical and rational reason why people behave in the ways they do.

I have a personal story I enjoy sharing with my audiences that perfectly illustrates the value of observing behaviors and having the clear ability to understand the motivation behind them. Marshall is my older son and Austin is my younger son. There's a four and a half year difference between them. They both like to play computer games. Marshall just happens to be a lot better at it (after all, he has had more years of practice!). In our study at home we have both of our computers networked and the boys can play with each other on the computer games.

One afternoon a little girl Austin's age who lives across the street came over. She sat and watched them play their computer game. After a while, I walked by the study and noticed Austin was not there. I went looking for him and found him in his room. When I asked him what he was doing in there, he spun around and I could see he was very upset.

"I'm not playing anymore," Austin shouted at me, "because Marshall's cheating and he's just not playing fair!"

Now, David, this is where the skills I've been referring to come in handy. Because I know this child's behavior styles, what motivates him, the underlying factors behind his stress behavior, and all the different pieces that come together with verbal and nonverbal communication with this child, I knew that the statement he expressed to me was not the real reason for what was upsetting him so much. It had nothing to do with Marshall playing fair or unfair.

Let me ask you, how many times have we been upset, and because we were emotional at the time, the behavior and language we used to express it (even those who choose to say nothing and keep it inside) didn't accurately portray the real underlying hurt or problem? So, if someone were to respond to what we were saying instead of what was truly the issue, we were left even more frustrated and upset than when we started.

Now, think about this: If I had reacted based solely on Austin's literal verbal communication, I could have done a couple of things: I could have gone to the study and gotten mad at Marshall for cheating and told him to get off the computer, or to punish him some way. If I had done either of those things, it wouldn't have been fair because he wasn't cheating. That would have chipped away at our relationship because I would have shown a lack of trust and I would have jumped on him unjustly.

Or, in response to this situation, I could have said to Austin, "This is really silly. It doesn't matter and you're upset over nothing. It's only a game. Get over it!" This would have dismissed what he felt was important and would not have validated his feelings. Responding in such a way would have chipped away at our relationship for the fact that I would have dismissed his needs. When this happens enough, there is a complete erosion of a relationship. The need to feel heard and validated is basic in human nature.

Wright

So, what did you do instead?

Ramsay

I knew first of all that it wasn't a matter of winning or losing in this game for Austin. That's not what is important to his personality type. What's important is that everybody gets along and has a good time. I also know the other part of his personality and his needs and wants is that of a perfectionist. The one thing perfectionists do not like and fear the most, is to show that they are not perfect. So when he swung around and said to me that he wasn't playing because Marshall was cheating, I knew that wasn't the real issue.

So, knowing the things I know, what I did was look at him and ask, "Austin, did Marshall embarrass you in front of your company?"

Ten words.

He just grinned. Right then he knew, without a doubt, that I understood—I had hit the nail on the head. His body visibly relaxed and I could see he was going to be just fine. With those ten words I showed him I understood him, I validated how he felt, and that's all it took.

Wright

Does this mean that you have to agree with someone when they are upset?

Ramsay

No, David, it doesn't. When I respond in this manner with someone, it doesn't mean I have to agree, it just means that I understand and validate what has upset or put stress on him or her.

How many of us have felt empty and frustrated when we are not validated and just callously dismissed by someone else? What does this do to our self-worth? How would this allow us to respect the other person who is doing the dismissing? And dismissing can often be coupled with a condescending attitude. Imagine how this world would be if just this one skill was used consistently in a positive way?

It's not *just* communication; it's the *right* communication.

Wright

I can see how, over a period of time, you might develop a real intuitive look at a family member but how do you get this understanding of other people?

Ramsay

The best way to do it is to listen and to observe. You have to know what you're looking and listening for. That's why in my program, "Working and Playing Well with Others," I share with people just how easy it is.

I can usually come to a pretty accurate understanding of someone I am interacting with within about thirty seconds. I can adapt what it is I am saying and especially *how* I am saying it.

There are some people who do not want you very close to them physically—they are not comfortable with that, they don't want you to invade their personal space. With other people, within minutes of meeting them, you can hug and be best friends—it just clicks. You have to be able to discern the difference quickly.

Wright

Is it really all that important?

Ramsay

It's extremely important. I ask my clients to consider what it costs them to have higher stress and less productivity in their company or to miss crucial verbal and nonverbal cues altogether whether it's with coworkers or customers. I mean true, dollar figure cost. It's staggering!

Let's take negotiating for example. Based on what the other person's behavior style is will determine the style of their negotiating approach. For instance, there are those who feel that "peace at any price" is the way to go because they fear conflict. Someone could really take unfair advantage of this kind of person! Is this who you would pick to negotiate for your business? Other people want glory and recognition for their negotiating skills, while still others want to blaze on with an overwhelming and decisive victory no matter what, and they don't care what carnage they leave behind them! Others are very logical and factual and they will think a lot less of those who do not come to the table with all their facts and figures in line. So negotiating styles are completely different with each behavioral style.

This is crucial information to have going into business discussions and could give someone an advantage if they had these observation and communication skills.

Wright

Is this skill hard to learn?

Ramsay

Not at all—it is not hard at all to learn! I explain the dynamics of relationships and how understanding the difference between one personality and another can better equip you in your professional dealings.

I get so excited about sharing this information because when explained in an easy to understand way, it's not hard at all! It all makes sense! Then when it all ties back together it's very clear why there are some people we just don't hit it off with. I explain why that happens and what can be done to help neutralize it.

The response and feedback I continually receive from my audiences is that I make the concept of understanding people so easy to identify with and comprehend. I share information in my workshops in a way that is fun, informative, interactive, and most of all—never boring! I am trained in the four styles of Adult Learning and Rapid Course Design and am aware of the four critical phases of the adult learning process, which I integrate into every workshop and training I design.

I received a written testimonial given to me by one woman who gave me permission to use it. She said, "Now I understand why my boss and I butt heads and it is easier to accept." It didn't mean it was going to change but now she understood and with understanding came power. That ties back in to personal power of relationships.

Wright

Okay! You also mentioned "being adaptable" as the second part of developing personal power. Would you tell our readers a little bit about that?

Ramsay

The art of being adaptable is another type of skill used in verbal and nonverbal communication. What that means is that you are willing to be accommodating to others to get the best out of them for the situation.

I think you'd agree that we behave differently when we're in our workspace versus playing poker with our friends, or being part of a church or volunteer group. We play different roles in our lives. We might be assertive lions at the office because we are supposed to be, but we're lambs at home because we prefer to be. That's just how it is—we play different roles.

Being adaptable is useful because if you're not willing to listen, observe, and make the fine distinctions and changes you need to make to ensure a successful relationship, then it's not going to be helpful in the long run.

Wright

So if I'm hearing you correctly, being adaptable is really not "giving in," is it?

Ramsay

No not at all. By treating every single person the same way, you are going to get dismal results. You're alienating three quarters of the population out there! You would be much more effective if you have a willingness to be adaptable.

Wright

Giving in is such a negative term.

Ramsay

Let's look at some examples. We've all been an upset customer because of some experience we had at some point in our life somewhere. When we go in and we're upset about a product or a service we didn't get and all we hear is, "Well, that's our company policy," or, "I'm sorry, but we don't do that," or we're met with an air of indifference or even complete silence, it's just more infuriating. That person should have been more adaptable and listened to our complaint, acted like they understood, had a bit of empathy, and *then* explained the situation and either fixed it or explained why they couldn't or why it happened the way it did. That's not giving in; it's being adaptable and caring enough to understand what the customer is saying. That's called good customer service—something which, by the way, is fast disappearing.

Wright

Do you have any final words of advice or encouragement about developing personal power?

Ramsay

We can adapt to and communicate in styles that meet the needs of others and that's when we can have the most influence over a group. That's where the personal power comes from.

It's simple, but it's not easy—it's one of those things that must be continually in our head; it takes practice.

Using the skills I have been talking about can help diffuse conflicts, help deal successfully with different types of people, help provide stellar service to clients, and even close a higher ratio of sales!

This is where knowledge is power and communication is key but it has to be the *right* kind of knowledge that provides personal power and the communication has to be the *right* kind of communication.

Wright

I can imagine you have a lot of goals with personal power but I heard you use the word "influence." Would you consider that to be the most important goal of personal power?

Ramsay

Influence is one of them. A higher level of understanding is another. Because, again, personal power doesn't come from position, it comes from the ability to influence those around you and to inspire them to work as a cohesive team to carry out goals. It takes effort and practice. With practice comes habit.

Wright

What a great conversation. You're a very interesting speaker; I can't wait to hear you on the platform one of these days.

Ramsay

I really appreciate that! I love speaking with people, making them laugh, and sharing crucial information that could instantly make a positive impact in their lives.

David, I really enjoyed our conversation today. Thank you.

Wright

Today we've been talking with Beth Marshall Ramsay. She is a business relationship expert and humorist. She is also a professional level member of the National Speakers Association. She captivates her audience through her humorous and entertaining style. As we have found out today she has given us a lot of practical tips.

Thank you so much, Beth, for being with us today on *Pillars of Success*.

About the Author

BETH MARSHALL RAMSAY captivates audiences through her humorous and entertaining style while sharing crucial tips, tools, and information that positively impacts the bottom line, improves customer service, increases sales, and promotes harmony in the work environment. Beth shares exactly why people do what they do, what simple things that can be done to understand it, neutralize it, and work with it to improve relationships instantly.

Beth is known for turning complex subject matter into fun and useful knowledge for her audiences in an "EZ2" understand way. Her most requested presentation is "Working and Playing Well With Others" in which she shares ways to reduce stress, motivate others and capitalize on the strengths of individuals.

Her philosophy of "If it's not fun, I'm going to be hard-pressed to learn it" has motivated her to help those in search of "EZ2" understand concepts, critical in improving their daily lives and interactions with others. An experienced corporate trainer, Beth is also certified in the method of Adult Accelerated Learning and Rapid Course Design, which addresses the specific needs of the adult learner.

Beth Marshall Ramsay
EZ2 Enterprises
6175 SE 13th Avenue
Ocala, FL 34480
Phone: 239.851.2577 (direct)
E-mail: EZ2Enterprises@earthlink.net
www.EZ2Enterprises.com

Chapter Seven

PETER SCHOR

THE INTERVIEW

David Wright (Wright)

Today we're talking with Peter Schor. A writer, speaker, and trainer, Peter has inspired and motivated over 450,000 businessmen and women throughout the U.S., Canada, Western Europe, and Asia. He has received numerous national industry awards, serves as a brand strategist for many companies, he is a popular columnist for magazines and a freelance writer for many others. Peter is also an expert in consulting, coaching clients in the field of sales, marketing, and public relations. Peter's compelling presentations inspire people to discover the best in themselves and rediscover their zest for living. Peter says, "Some people are 'lucky.'" He defines L-U-C-K as: "Labor Under Correct Knowledge."

Peter, welcome to *Pillars of Success*.

Peter Schor (Schor)

Thank you David.

Wright

How tell me, how did you become an expert on positive attitude?

Schor

The first thirty-five years of my life I had a negative and pessimistic attitude. I called it "stinkin' thinking." I was very unhappy and bottomed out but I knew there was a better way. I decided to attend many, many personal growth seminars that challenged me from rappelling down mountains to climbing and standing on top of a telephone pole in a harness, all in order to push my limits of growing personally. During this last twenty-year span I became a "junkie" of learning about all types of human behavior including positive attitudes.

I have read and listened to more than 650 books and audiotapes and I've done about 150 live seminars.

Wright

So you believe 100 percent that one's attitude controls everything. How do you define a positive attitude?

Schor

I do. I totally believe that it is the absolute truth. An attitude is an allegory of seeing the glass half empty or half full. There are most likely three distinctive attitudes or expectations when someone picks up something to read like this or takes in new information:

1. Why am I reading this information?
2. Perhaps I will learn something from this.
3. I will devour this information and change my life.

It's all choice—everyone has a choice to do that. But positive attitudes control our expectations and the outcomes. No one rises to low expectations. It's our choice to be proactive or reactive to everything around us.

A recent book, *Learned Optimism*, by Martin E. P. Seligman, PhD, came from fifty years of research, both private and government. In it he states, "It's a proven fact that optimistic people live 20 percent longer than pessimistic people." This is double-blinded study information.

Wright

Why are positive attitudes thought by many people as being short term?

Schor

That's interesting because a couple of years ago, Zig Ziglar, the master motivator and attitude guru, was interviewed for a national television news show. I saw the videotape. The interviewer said, "Zig, motivation is not permanent. It's never worked long-term."

Zig responded from his Southern Christian heart saying, "You're absolutely, 100 percent right."

You could see the interviewer's face look victorious until Zig said, "Neither is bathing permanent, but if you bathe every day you'll smell good."

Many of us are taught that it's important to work out physically each day to stay in shape. Many of us are taught to work smarter— not necessarily harder but smarter; but what about working out for fifteen minutes every day when we wake up in the morning? Wouldn't that be a more proactive approach to meeting the challenges of every day? What happens is, people think of motivation as something they do once a year. That would be like going to the gym once a year and expect to be in good shape. I see people attend a full day, eight-hour seminar, get done with the seminar and are pumped up, go out to their car or truck, they have a flat tire and it wipes out the entire eight-hour motivational day. That's not what motivation is. It's a lot more and more in depth.

Wright

I've heard you say it is hard to shift your attitude from negative to positive without understanding how to "embrace change"?

Schor

The key issue behind people wanting to know how to do it is knowing how to embrace change. Scientists have proven that it takes twenty-one repetitive days to change a habit or start a new one. The use of what I call "trigger devices—a word or phrase that helps you remember what you need to do—daily for twenty-one days helps you create the desire to change or a new habit. I've put these words on my mirror in the bathroom, on the refrigerator, on the dashboard in my car, and on my desk just as a trigger to remind me for twenty-one days to either start a new habit or change an old one.

Taking in information is important. I find there are three distinctive ways to take in new or foreign information. You can agree or disagree and when you disagree you have to confront that in conversation or in research.

The third way is the way the happiest, most motivated and successful people do it and it is just to be open. They are open to saying, "Alright, this is new information. It doesn't match what I currently believe but is it something I need to take a look at?" I think open people can evolve and move on in their life.

The last part is understanding the adult learning curve on how we as adults retain information. We retain 10 percent of what we read, 20 percent of what we hear, 30 percent of what we see, 50 percent when we hear it and see it, and 70 percent when it's repeated, then 90 percent when it's repeated and performed. That's why people will go to a movie on Saturday night and when someone in the office on Monday will ask what movie they saw they can hardly remember the movie unless it made an extreme impact. This is because seeing it without repeating it or doing more than that doesn't make that information stick or change a habit.

Wright

How easily can one change from having a negative attitude to having a positive attitude?

Schor

It's very simple to understand and implement by using some good tools. In reading hundreds of books on attitude and others' philosophies I've found there's a way to simplify this so that the everyday person can change his or her attitude and become a positive thinker.

I call the conscious mind "the boss." This is the level where I'm reading the information.

I call the subconscious mind the "genie" or the "computer." The subconscious mind is where everything we have ever seen, heard, or experienced in our life is stored. The genie/computer only responds to whatever you tell it. If you say you think you're coming down with a cold, the genie says okay. The conscious mind—the boss—is what controls the whole scenario. The boss is in control of the genie/computer, regardless of what we have in there—whatever our life's experiences are, up to this very moment, right now. We can reprogram our genie/computer with the use of some proven methods.

I came up with four distinctive methods that most people will agree upon as really excellent tools for working out:

1. *Affirmations*—These are called expectations in today's sales world. Affirmations are positive statements that, when re-

peated frequently to your genie/computer, creates desired results especially when putting emotion into it, etc. There are many books available on affirmations.

2. *Subliminal tapes*—These are taped messages that go directly into the genie/computer mind, bypassing the conscious mind while you're sleeping. These are sold in bookstores under a wide variety of titles. A good example of subliminal tapes is the Berlitz Language Tapes that have been advertised consistently in magazines for many years. There's a 100 percent unconditional guarantee that if you follow their guidelines it will work. In the fine print it states, "80 percent subconscious learning and 20 percent conscious learning."

3. *Selective listening*—Be selective with the input that goes into your genie/computer. For twenty-one days be conscious of what you're going to listen to and not send it to your computer unless it's going to be for your good. We get our daily information from television, radio, newspapers, music, etc. Most of it is a negative deposit so unless we selectively listen we can send bad information to the genie/computer. The worst thing to do (I call it "mental suicide") is leaving the television set on when you go to sleep. They've found out that there's no conscious screening of that information and it causes people to have the same response—they wake up tired, they feel they've worked a week without sleeping, or they think they're coming down with a cold or a virus. It'd just not a good thing to do.

4. *Selective communication*—I call this self-talk. Scientific researchers have proven that we talk at the rate of 500 words a minute. Negative self-talk such as, "How did I ever get into my field of business? We're in a recession; my prices are too high. I can't do it, etc." This is self-talk that is defeating. Repeated over and over again it becomes hypnotic. Reactive language such as, "I have to," or, "I should," or, "I must," can be changed to proactive language such as, "I choose to," "I will," "I prefer," etc. Wouldn't it be better to say, "I choose to go to work," for twenty-one repetitive days rather than, "I have to go to work."

If we want to take a look at the mind in a scientific manner, which a lot of people reading this will do, take a look at thoughts at the conscious level. These thoughts become feelings at the subconscious level and result in a change of the behavior. Thoughts become feelings and feelings become your behavior.

Wright

So how can we maintain a positive attitude in a negative, toxic world?

Schor

I've come up with a fifteen-minute, daily workout. The framework of this workout can be centered on people's own personal goals and their life—where they want to be and who they are.

I've developed this workout where I wake up in the morning and read the desk calendar for the day. I read a message and stay with that message for one minute. I read it and I read it again. I think about how it pertains to this day. Then I take another desk calendar called "I Use Giant Steps," by Anthony Robbins. It contains 365 daily lessons. I read that for a minute. I then read a daily creative thought book. It could be religious or nonreligious but it should be spiritual and I read that for two minutes. It could be, for anyone, the Bible where you read a passage for two minutes and you apply that and consider how it works for you that day. Then I have a three-minute workout where I use my affirmations to support my written goals. Then for six minutes I review my written goals for all areas of my life and during the last two minutes of the workout is when I focus on that day's work toward my goals.

I think everyone can come up with some sort of workout. We all know that life happens and we have to be flexible with this but when we do a workout the chances of having a better day are greater than not doing it at all.

Wright

Will you tell our readers about how stress and poor time management affects our positive attitude?

Schor

The number one most profound time management tip that increases time and reduces stress is to realize that you will never, ever, ever, ever get caught up!

Wright

I think I'll just shoot myself right now!

Schor

The first time I heard that it was an Aha! for me that knocked me back for days. I contemplated what it really meant and I think within days it cut down at least 50 percent of my stress. Our daily lives are filled with so many repetitive tasks—showering in the morning, getting dressed, eating, grocery shopping, answering the telephone, driving to work, etc. We never really get "caught up." I want readers to seriously reflect on what this means before we move on.

Those who will ponder this and understand its significance will find their stress levels are reduced and their time will be increased. Stress cuts down on our effectiveness to manage our time. Reducing stress creates a positive attitude.

Wright

How does having goals effect positive attitudes?

Schor

Writing down goals is the most important thing we can do for ourselves. Some people don't like the word "goals," so I use the word "dreams." Stress and a negative attitude are caused by not doing what you really want to do in life.

I believe we need to check in with ourselves from time to time with self-probing questions like, "Am I enrolled in someone else's movie, life or goal, or am I in my own movie?" Another question to ask is, "What would I do with my life if I knew I could not fail?"

Not having written goals is another reason why we get stressed. You can't hit the target if you can't see it. Failing to plan is planning to fail. The feeling of not being in control of life adds to stress and creates a negative attitude.

Wright

Who are some of your favorite and most inspiring motivational speakers?

Schor

There are so many of them. Being that I've taken in over eight hundred books, tapes, and live seminars in behavior, especially in attitude, here are some of my favorites that come to mind. Everybody is different in life and I celebrate that diversity but these are people who resonate with me.

My number one favorite is Jim Rohn. There is something about Jim and the way he writes and the information he gives, especially in his book, *The Art of Exceptional Living.*

The second one I would have to say is Zig Ziglar. From the first time I read *See You at the Top* and *A View at the Top* and just from following the information he has put out, I'd have to put Zig in the second spot.

The third one is Anthony Robbins author of *Unlimited Power* and *Awakening the Giant Within.* Those are two very powerful books he's put out along with many other things. I have a tremendous amount of respect for him.

The fourth one would be author Og Mandino. *The Secrets of Success and Happiness* is one of my favorites that comes to mind. Og, may he rest in peace, has contributed so much to human potential and should be acknowledged all the time.

One of the authors not many people have read is a gentleman named Alan H. Cohen. Alan has written approximately eighteen books including: *The Dragon Doesn't Live Here Anymore* and *Why Your Life Sucks and What You Can Do About it.* He uses some humorous anecdotes—stories that really connect people to attitude and living life to its fullest. He is a "heart-centered writer and speaker" like myself.

Winding down my list I have to put Jack Canfield in there. His book, *How to Build Self-esteem* is one of my favorites of his.

A couple of others include Dr. Wayne W. Dyer's *The Secrets of the Power of Intention* is probably the hottest book I have ever read and heard along with his classic book, *You'll See It When You Believe It,* was one of the first books I read of his.

Stephen Covey's *7 Habits . . .* and *First Things First*—I couldn't leave him out and probably the last person who comes to mind who inspires me (but I could go on) is Brian Tracey. Brian does so many wonderful things.

Wright

Out of the eight living people you listed, seven of them have been in our books, so you've got great taste.

Schor

Thank you. There are so many wonderful people out there but you know, it's always good to pick up a book or attend a seminar and be assured that the person writing the book or who is presenting the seminar has lived it or has proven models of it rather than after you've read it to find the book was a recall or the information isn't accurate after you try to use it.

Wright

Knowing how disciplined you are and how goal-oriented you are and how you absorb information you get from others, would you share with our readers—and I know you must have one—a favorite all-time quote about positive attitude?

Schor

I do have one that is my favorite. When I saw it I knew it had to be the top quote and it still is. It was written by Frank Outlaw who said, "Watch your thoughts, they become words. Watch your words, they become actions. Watch your actions, they become habits. Watch your habits, they become character. Watch your character, it becomes your destiny." That is my number one favorite.

I know by embracing change that change is inevitable and growth is optional and I see life as a journey not a destination. I always remember one thing to be true: attitude is everything.

Wright

What a great conversation, Peter. You know how much I always love talking with you.

Schor

I enjoy what I do. I was doing five cities in five days in Florida two weeks ago. I went from Jacksonville to Orlando to Tampa to West Palm Beach and then to the Miami area. I repeated the same program each time. It was a six-hour program. By the time I packed up and drove to the next one and set up the room I'd had maybe five or six hours of sleep. The person who hired me came the first day to make sure that everything was going to be set up right and to my liking and so forth. He was there maybe an hour. On the last day he came to pay me the balance for the five seminars. He stayed the entire day. After the day was over he told me how much collectively the close to a thousand people who attended the seminars appreciated the program.

He had one question and asked, "I don't know if I could do this. I was there the first day and you had an incredible amount of enthusiasm. You had the audience alive and it was just incredible. Then the last day you were still able to keep the same intensity. You were doing the same program and yet you were doing it as though it was the first time you've ever done it. How do you do that?"

I told him, "You know the information was the same, but every day it was a new group of people and I knew that and with each new group I could make a difference in their lives. I was all about making that difference. It wasn't the outcome of getting paid, it was the fact that every day felt like the first day." He understood what I meant. It was the passion and love for helping other people that inspired me to keep it fresh.

Wright

I really do appreciate your spending all this time with me today answering all these questions. I know I have learned a lot and I'm sure our readers will.

Today we have been talking with Peter Schor. He is a writer, speaker, and trainer. He's also an expert in consulting, coaching clients in the fields of sales, marketing, and public relations. As we have found out today, his compelling presentations do indeed inspire people to discover the very best in themselves and rediscover, in many cases, their zest for living.

Peter, thank you so much for being with us today on *Pillars of Success.*

About The Author

A writer, speaker, and trainer, Peter has inspired and motivated over 450,000 businessmen and women throughout the U.S., Canada, Western Europe, and Asia. He has received numerous national industry awards, serves as a brand strategist for many companies, and he is a popular columnist for magazines and a freelance writer for many others. Peter is also an expert in consulting, coaching clients in the field of sales, marketing, and public relations. Peter's compelling presentations inspire people to discover the best in themselves and rediscover their zest for living. Peter says, "Some people are 'lucky.' " He defines L-U-C-K as: "Labor Under Correct Knowledge."

Peter Schor

Dynamic Results, Inc.

1491 Ivy Arbor Lane

Lincoln, CA 95648

Phone: 916.408.5346

Fax: 916.408.5899

E-mail: pschor@dynamicresultsinc.com

www.dynamicresultsonline.com

Chapter Eight

JIM ROHN

David E. Wright (Wright)

It is my sincere pleasure today to welcome Jim Rohn to *Pillars of Success*. Jim has been described as everything from a master motivator to a modern-day Will Rogers to a legend. Jim has been internationally hailed as one of the most influential thinkers of our time. His professional development seminars have spanned thirty-nine years. He has addressed more than 6,000 audiences and four million people worldwide. He has authored seventeen different books as well as dozens of audio and video programs. There simply aren't enough superlatives when introducing Jim Rohn.

Jim, thank you for taking the time to visit with us today.

Jim Rohn (Rohn)

Thanks for that introduction. I appreciate that.

Wright

I'd say those four million people just went up. You just told me that you'd been in Asia for a few weeks.

Rohn

Yes, I just finished lecturing in seven countries during the last three weeks in May, so I've been busy.

Wright

Did you speak to a lot of people?

Rohn

A *lot* of people.

Wright

We have titled this program and book *Pillars of Success* because we believe there are bedrock issues related to personal development and success—things that everyone must have to support their lives and to build success upon. Your life has been built around these kinds of bedrock principles and I'm eager to let you begin telling us about them. Can we start with character? In your book, *Cultivating an Unshakable Character*, you described "twelve pillars of character." Rather than dealing with those specifically, will you just touch on character and tell us how character applies to personal development and success?

Rohn

Character suggests loyalty. Character suggests building reputation. Character is something that shows outside because you've worked on it on the inside. I think the first thing is to resolve somewhere along the way is a frame of mind that says, "I really want to be a person of character in my business as well as in my personal life. Having those qualities that make for success and also make for an attractive person in the marketplace or in the community, in politics, religion, whatever it is."

We probably know ourselves better than anyone else does. Conscience is a pretty good guide as to whether we sometimes get off track and finally get back on. We're all inclined to make some mistakes. A longtime dear friend of mine who built an incredible success story has a list of virtues that was so long it easily overcame his list of mistakes. He made his share of mistakes and I've made my share, but I think a good character should be the objective and purpose for all of us as far as our lives are concerned so that we can live comfortably with ourselves and we can enjoy high self-esteem. The ultimate goal is to keep your list of virtues growing and developing so that it will overcome your list of mistakes.

During the course of a lifetime we experience challenges every day. The temptations are there constantly. I tell the Bible story of two nice people, not one bad person and one good person, but two nice people according to the storyteller. The story includes the word, "However" and, you know, the word "however" begins the whole drama of life. I call it, "the mystery and the magic." You describe an opportunity to two different people and one sees it and the other one doesn't see it. Sometimes that confuses us, but that's what life is. The one who see it sees the magic. The one who doesn't see it; that's the mystery.

There were two nice people, however, in just a brief description it says one built his house on the rock and the other built his house on the sand. (See Matthew 7:24–27.) Almost instantaneously one recognizes the situation—wow! The one who built his house on the sand is in trouble! Sure enough, the storyteller says the storms came, as they always do. The one who built his house on the rock was saved and the one who built his house on the sand was lost. What an instant, quick little story to illustrate how we must all be positive; but also wise and careful. What it suggests is that even nice people can make careless decisions and can also make foolish decisions. Even a person of character still has to watch.

Sometimes a foolish decision can be fatal. Here in Los Angeles a guy's in a hurry for appointment. He's a nice guy, a good father. He loves his family. He's a good citizen of the community. This is a nice guy, but in his hurry to get to an appointment he comes to the intersection, the light turns red, and some voice in his head says, "Go ahead; you're late. You can make it this time." Now he is dead—he's a fatality. You don't have to go off to some foreign war to lose your life. All you have to do is make a foolish or careless decision at the wrong moment in time. The key is to stay on track.

I have a good saying, "Everything by longevity tends to get off course." It doesn't matter whether it's a marriage, a friendship, or a business, or working with someone. Over a period of time everything sort of erodes in terms of line of direction. On the way to the moon the early astronauts had to make what they called midcourse corrections. Solar winds they didn't anticipate would blow them a little bit off course. As they noticed those deviations in course, they had to use onboard propulsion systems to fire either the forward facing thrusters or rear facing thrusters to get back on course. Course corrections were especially important during NASA's lunar missions—you can't miss the moon, right? If you're flying you can miss St. Louis and hit Chicago and you're still okay, but you can't miss the moon because if you do, you can't get back!

This is a simple demonstration indicating that some destinations are critical. What it also illustrates is that by longevity things tend to get off course. If it's been going for a while, maybe you're okay, but sure enough, inevitably, whatever it is, whether it's circumstances or temptations, or if we just need a breather and need to relax, you're going to deviate off course if you don't make course corrections. The seventh day out of the seven days of the week was called the day of rest. Six days labor; one day rest. You have to make sure you don't rest another day, or an extra day, or too long because if you rest too long the weeds take the garden. Not to think so is naïve, so we have to keep working on character—being a person of our word to the best of our ability speaking the truth. Character says you can count on me. If you send me off on the other side of the world to do a project, don't worry about it because I'm there. If someone says, "Jim Rohn is in Japan and he's conducting a series of lectures to some very important client of ours," hopefully my reputation is such that they can sleep like a baby because they have confidence that I'm there—I'll take care of it. I'm not going to show up drunk. I'm going to be careful about my reputation. All of that is constant, even in what may seem the little matters that have to do with the value of our lives.

Just this morning that little voice in my head said, *"You're running a little bit late; you don't have to do your exercises this morning."* Sure enough, Jim Rohn, as well as everyone else, has got to resist that little voice and say, "No, no," and fall on the floor and do the pushups and the crunches and the usual routine things to stay healthy. I'll be seventy-five in September so I just have to resist the temptation to relax a little bit and take it a little easier. We all need to relax and take it easy, but not too long.

You've got to guard against making foolish decisions. Maybe the first day there are no consequences, or the first ninety days, or the first year, but over time errors in judgment build and erode our character and our reputation and the things we consider valuable. But I think character is being conscious every day as best you can about what we do because temptations are constant every day. At the coffee shop, the waitress gives you the wrong change. It's easy to be short and say, "This shouldn't happen." In those little moments you have the choice of whether to be kind, or not to say anything and let it go.

Those moments of decision happen every day, whether it's running the red light or being short with the waitress at the coffee shop. I think a person of character tries to be more consciously aware of these moments so that they don't let anything get too far off course.

Wright

I noticed a program on your Web site called *The Day That Turns Your Life Around*. You talk about how just one day can turn any *what if* into *what is*. How in the world can someone change in just one day?

Rohn

I suggest when people who are involved in training and going to lectures and seminars, go to everything you possibly can—within reason. Some of those occasions can be life changing. You look back and say, *"Wow! I was never the same after that occasion."* You have to go to as many quality lectures as you can. The early Christians were told, *"Don't neglect their assemblies. We're brand new and every time we meet together is very important."* (See Hebrews 10:25.) So don't neglect and don't pass. Just because you think, *"Well I've been to those so I know what they're all about,"* go to all of them. I've found that especially to be true. Some occasion will just turn your life around. It's like having four numbers you need to dial into a lock in order to open it up. You go to one class and it's standard. You go to another sermon and it's fairly ordinary. You go to something else and it's routine. And then you go to the fourth one, sure enough, the fourth one you attend you hear something that just turns your light on; whether it's a sentence or an entire sermon; but that particular day the timing was right, the atmosphere was right, and you were right. Sure enough, a light went on, something within you was triggered, and as you look back you think, *"Wow, that was one of those days that made an extraordinary difference in the quality of my life and my future."*

Wright

I remember back in the '60s when I was a much, much younger fellow, I listened to a Methodist minister who was a good friend of mine. I had heard him speak hundreds of times, but on this occasion we were talking about issues of decision-making, character building, and all that sort of thing in a private conversation. He told me, "David some things are right even if no one does it and some things are wrong even if everyone does it." That was a life-altering experience for me.

Rohn

Something that gives you a better fix on a compass—on a reading—and you get it in a moment is that life changing experience. You might get it in a sermon or by way of an experience, but it serves you the rest of your life. It's something that just drops into your consciousness, whether it's a book, a movie, a sermon, or a conversation with a friend, any one of these can bring you a life changing experience. That experience will cause you to look at life in a certain new way and will help you to better judge things during the rest of your life. Before then you had difficulty, but after that moment or that day, sure enough, it just helps to improve the quality of all the systems of your life.

Wright

I overheard a conversation recently in which a businessman mentioned how ambitious one of his employees was, but his tone of voice made it sound as if this person's ambition was a character flaw, almost like being dishonest. What do you think about ambition? Is it a necessary component of a successful life?

Rohn

It's absolutely necessary. Who knows why one person is more ambitious than another? Here's a marketing system that allows you to start at the bottom and go to the top; why wouldn't everyone strive for that? Some people want to live a more serene life. Others find within them something that burns to conquer the world. It's not a matter of the degree of ambition; legitimate ambition is hoping to gain something valuable in the service of others, whereas on the wrong side of ambition is greed striving benefit at the expense of others.

I think that's been a pretty good guideline for me to follow. I have to ask myself what I'm trying to get someone to do? Am I hoping that person will do something at his or her expense so that I will gain, or am I truly rendering a service to direct someone toward a better life? That's a good guideline—hoping to gain by serving others, not at the expense of others.

Zig Ziglar states the old success law very well, "*If you help enough people get what they want, you can have everything you want.*" When I first heard that about forty-five years ago I underlined the word *everything* and thought it worth going for. I thought, "Let's see if I can find a way to give service to many people—help them get what they need and what they want, and then that will take care of me." That philosophy certainly has worked for me, and it will work for anyone.

Regarding ambition, I don't know, sometimes a person goes along for a while and then something clicks, something turns on, or they find the right colleague. I've had that happen to me several times during the course of my life where someone said, "Come with me; let's go," and sure enough, it turned out to be a great, rewarding experience. What I would have done if that person or these people had not come along and said, "Come along; go with us. Let's do something extraordinary," who knows? I don't know what I would have done in the absence of that. Probably something else would have attracted me. There's something powerful in the expression *"Let's go do it."* Some things are really tough to do all by yourself, but then somebody says, *"Let's go start our exercise program,"* or, *"Let's get healthy,"* or, *"Let's start a business,"* or, *"Let's develop this product and take it around the world,"* and off you go.

I picked up on a phrase from the Bible (Ecclesiastes 4:12) that says, ". . . a threefold cord is not quickly broken." If two or three agree on a common purpose, nothing is impossible. I picked up on that and it's really true. By yourself you don't usually say, "I'm going to go conquer the world." If you've got two or three who agree with you, it might make the difference—*"We're going to take this around the world. We're going to do something extraordinary."* It's always in the *"we"*—two, three, four, or a few. If they have a common purpose they can do extraordinary things.

Wright

I remember back in the middle '70s one of the business mentors in my life down in Waco, Texas, introduced me to the concept of self-imposed limitations. I noticed in your program, *The Art of Exceptional Living,* you explain four major lessons one must master to overcome self-imposed restrictions. I don't want you to have to recall those things, but can you touch on self-imposed restrictions briefly and describe the kinds of restrictions people may deal with in their personal and professional lives?

Rohn

Some of that comes early. When you were told as child that you couldn't do something, or that you were too short, or you were too tall, or you were too young, that voice will become a part of our way of thinking. I use the phrase, *"Don't become a victim of yourself."* We have to sort out our own thinking. Beware of the thief on the street who's after your purse, but also beware of the thief in your mind who's after your promise. That mental thief will say, *"You've never done it before; what makes you think you can do it now? It's going to work for them, but it's not going to work for you. They got in early; you're too late."* Everyone goes through that thinking challenge and that's where some of it comes from. Perhaps we've picked up what someone has said and that negative part of our life has picked it up and tried to convince us that it's true.

This is where contemplation—thinking—reading, and spending some fairly consistent time examining your own thoughts comes in so that you line up on the positive side. I'm personally using this concept now fairly consistently (I did it during my lecture tour of the seven countries recently)—opposites are in conflict and we're in the middle. This describes life and life's adventure about as well as it can be described.

This whole conflict, according to one storyteller started early when God created the angels. He gave them the dignity and privilege of choice. Sure enough, a third of them conspired with Lucifer, according to the storyteller, to take over God's throne. They didn't make it; they got thrown down. But back then was when this contest between the Creator and the spoiler began (see Revelation 12:6–8). That's still an image in our lives—the positive and the negative at war—negative trying to overcome positive.

If you keep developing positive, you can push the negative into a small corner. Illness tries to overcome your health—if you neglect your health plan, illness pushes and pushes and sure enough, you haven't got much health left. But if you work on your health, you can push and push, and you haven't got much illness left. It's a continual battle of light against darkness—tyranny against liberty.

For so long the world was ruled by tyranny. Finally the walls came down in Berlin. I was there last year seeing it one more time. Communism was on the run. Within what seems like a short period of time there's more liberty than tyranny now. Years ago when I used to go to South America, every country had a dictator. Now they're all gone.

Even in our own lives, sometimes for a while there's more difficulty than opportunity. Then it turns and we find more opportunity than difficulty. But you have to keep up a relentless pressure. You've got to keep working on your health. You can't just do it once, fix it, and it's done. It doesn't matter whether it's nutrition, exercise, moderation, or whatever it is, you keep that positive side exerting constant pressure on the negative because the negative is not going to go entirely away.

For example do you weed the garden one spring day after you've planted the crop you don't weed again during the entire growing season? The answer is no! You weed the garden and sure enough, you just turn your back for a little while and the weeds are growing again. You wonder how long this lasts, and the answer is until you've finally harvested your crop. If you want a good harvest come harvest time, you have to keep up this daily work of weeding all summer. I consider it like a mother gives nourishment to her child and the protection a father gives. If you just do the work of mother, survival isn't guaranteed. You have to do both—you have to protect *and* nourish.

Even in our own personal lives we have to work on the positive, whether it's health or relationships, or in business, or working with people. We have to be constantly on the alert for the encroachment, the push—the ever-relentless push of the negative that is liable to take it all. If you do a good job nourishing the positive, being vigilant about the negative, within this effort you'll find the chance to live a good life.

It never goes away—darkness is always striving to take over the light. If light burns brightly it eliminates the darkness. If it starts to get weak the darkness moves in; whether it's liberty and tyranny, or health and illness, or good and evil. That's why the old prophet said, "Hate the evil and love the good."—Amos 5:15. It's something you've got to choose daily. Be aware of the encroachment of that which is out to diminish, or eliminate, or erode the good values you have.

There's plenty of joy and success and fortune and positive-ness in your life that can be extraordinary in terms of lifestyle if you work at it and take care of the details. Just make sure you work on your character—that's the whole key—every day be watchful and mind the details.

Wright

Before we wrap up today I was hoping we could touch on your philosophy of living an inspired life. Some people scoff at the idea of inspiration being a key component to success and happiness, but you've written a 450-page book on the subject. What do you mean by "living an inspired life"?

Rohn

When I was growing up I had the benefit of being inspired by my faith—inspired by spirituality—thanks to my parents. They lived such a unique, inspiring life that I picked up on that. I remember early thinking, "Wow, I would like to be like them."

I've also been inspired by associations that I've had where the work others did, coupled with mine, created something unique. I'm inspired by possibilities. One of my business colleagues said, "If we do this right we can make a major contribution to the lives of millions of people." I thought, "Wow! I'm inspired by that." I never had a chance, up until my association with those people, to think I had a chance to make a contribution to millions of people's lives, but sure enough, it turned out to be possible. It turned out to be one of those unique things.

I'm inspired by what I do. For me the story never gets old, especially in business. At the age of twenty-five I met this extraordinary man who never went beyond the ninth grade in school. He never finished high school, never went to college or university, but he inspired me to know I could make changes in my life that would last forever. He inspired me to realize that one day I could be a person of reputation, that my success would create some honor and respect for myself. That turned out to be true. He said, "I promise you, Mr. Rohn, if you'll keep working like you're working now, developing your communication skills and all that, one of these days before walk into a room to speak, you'll hear someone say, *That's him; that's that famous man!*" Back then I thought, "Well, that could never happen for me."

Of the seven countries I just visited, the last one was Mexico. I just got back two days ago. I had an audience of about 2,000. Sure enough, as I walked in to get ready to make my presentation I heard someone say, "That's him; that's the famous man!" It just rang in my head from all those years ago when I was twenty-five years old (which was fifty years ago), my mentor had said, "This is going to happen if you keep growing and learning and challenging yourself to get better." I thought, "*Wow! Here it is; it's happened to me!*" That's inspiring.

What's also really inspiring is when your name appears in somebody's testimonial. "Here's the person who found me. Here's the person who got me started. Here's the person who wouldn't let me quit or who gave me more reasons for staying than for leaving. Here's the person who believed in me until I could believe in myself." And then they mention your name. That's one of the great rewards and that inspires me, even at my age. That's why I keep traveling the world sharing my story so that a year later or five years from now someone will say, "Jim Rohn just came to Japan back in 2005," or, "He just came to Singapore," or, "He just came to Taiwan," or, "He just came to Mexico. I was in the audience. Something clicked. Here's what's happened to me and to my family." And they mention my name. You can't buy that—you have to earn it. That inspires me.

Wright

I have a young friend who must be in his late thirties whom you have been inspiring now for the last ten years without knowing it. You are his mentor and his name is Steve Compton. He lives in Tennessee and he has taken those things you have taught him—specifically on videos and audiotapes—and he has followed them. He's a very, very successful businessman now, who comes from one of the most unlikely places. He has become a success and will say in a minute that those things he learned, he learned mainly from you.

I promised him I would ask you this question today. You've been using a journal for years and you even teach others how to use journals. So, as a final question, why has this been important to you and why do you feel that it's a critical tool for everyone?

Rohn

My mentor—the man I just talked about—got me started. Here's what he said, "Don't trust your memory." That just prompted me to write things down. He said, "If you hear a good idea, write it down." If it's a good health idea, record it. If it's a good spiritual idea—a sermon on a Sunday morning—write it down. Dr. Robert H. Schuller's son, Dr. Robert Anthony Schuller, gave one of the classic sermons of all time: *"Point One: If you think it's impossible, it isn't. Point Two: If you think you know everything, you don't. Point Three: If you think you're alone, you're not."* What a classic sermon! I took notes that day and I've still got them. That's what the journal is all about. Sometimes you're without your actual journal and you just take notes on a piece of paper, but when you get back home take it from the paper and put it in your journal. When you fill one up, just fill up another one, and then another one.

Mine are all going to go to my children and my grandchildren. It is a good source of the ideas that helped shape my life, my career, and my thinking. That's what it's for—to capture those things. Then, on a cold winter evening, sitting by the fire, you can go back through your journals and remind yourself about where you were when you heard this or that idea. It's refreshing. It's like listening to a song that thrilled you when you heard it ten years ago—when you listen to it again you get that same unique, extraordinary feeling.

Wright

As I started this, in the introduction I said there simply aren't enough superlatives when introducing you, Jim, and I make that statement again. There aren't enough superlatives to say anything when closing out a great interview like this. I do appreciate another fascinating interview and for sharing your insights and inspiration with us on *Pillars of Success*.

Rohn

It's always a pleasure for me. Thanks David, and give Steve Compton my best. Tell him I appreciate the compliment.

Wright

I certainly will. Thank you so much.

JIM ROHN knows the secrets of success—in business and in life. He has devoted his life to a study of the fundamentals of human behavior and personal motivation that affect professional performance. He can awaken the unlimited power of achievement within you! Jim Rohn simply cannot be described nor defined. Instead, he must be experienced. The remarkable combination of his personal style and his message does something to people that cannot be captured in a text description. The power that is behind his extraordinary effect on people is not found just in what he enables them to learn, but in what he makes them feel. Time spent with Jim Rohn, whether at a live seminar or through his audio and video programs, is an indescribable emotional journey that will expand your self-confidence, rekindle your determination to succeed and enrich your attitude—further intensifying your ambition to alter your life for the better.

Jim Rohn
www.jimrohn.com

Chapter Nine

NATHANIEL SCOTT, JR., MBA, RFC

David E. Wright (Wright)

Today we're talking with Nathaniel Scott, Jr., MBA, RFC. Nate began a distinguished career in the military as an enlisted man. He went on to graduate from West Point and became an Army Ranger with the rank of captain. He earned his bachelor's degree in engineering from the United States Military Academy and an MBA from George Washington University. He also completed an executive program in financial planning at Georgetown University. Prior to beginning a career as a financial advisor with the world's largest private wealth management firm, Nate built a net worth of over a million dollars on a very modest income with a $10,000 per month positive cash flow. He did this in just over fifteen months. Today, he owns over five million dollars in real estate properties. He is the president of DNA Business Services, which is a private consulting business offering Executive Coaching and Personal CFO services. In addition to church and family commitments, he serves as board president of Rebuilding Together Northeast Florida, a nonprofit organization whose mission is to preserve and revitalize houses and communities, assuring that low-income homeowners—particularly those who are elderly, disabled, or families with children—live in comfort, safety, and independence.

Nate, it's a pleasure to welcome you to *Pillars of Success*.

Nathaniel Scott, Jr. (Scott)

Thank you for this opportunity to share with you, David. It's a tremendous honor.

Wright

Many of the men and women I meet who have served in leadership roles in the military go on to great success in the private sector. Will you tell us a little bit more about your time in the service and describe how you used your experience and training to succeed in business?

Scott

Leadership is the most essential element of business. Leadership provides purpose, direction, and motivation in up and down markets. The leader determines the degree to which time and money are maximized, ensures these elements are effectively balanced, and decides how to use both in successfully accomplishing the mission of financial independence. My military career began as an enlisted soldier, which laid the groundwork for me as a leader. As an enlisted soldier, I was the follower and the doer. After serving three years as an enlisted soldier and after Desert Storm, I went on to West Point. When I graduated I was commissioned as an Army infantry officer. In this role, I was the leader, teacher, and doer. Fortunately, I had the experience of being the doer first, which gave me immediate credibility as a leader.

The principles I gained as an enlisted soldier as well as an officer were modeled after Army Field Manual 22–100—Army Leadership. Application of those principles helped me to be successful throughout my military career as well as in the business world. Here is the framework:

(1) **BE:**

(a) **TECHNICALLY AND TACTICALLY PROFICIENT:** Can accomplish all tasks to standard that are required to accomplish the mission. In real estate those tasks include market research and analysis, debt management, property management, financial proposal presentation, and capital formulation.

(b) **POSSESS PROFESSIONAL CHARACTER TRAITS:** Courage, Commitment, Candor, Competence, and Integrity.

(2) **KNOW**:

(a) Four major factors of leadership and how they affect each other: Those who are Led (Bank, Investors, Team, Support Network), The Leader (You or your Entity), The Situation (Market/Opportunity), and Communications.

(b) Yourself and seek self-improvement: Strengths and weaknesses of your character, knowledge, and skills. Continually develop your strengths and work on overcoming your weaknesses.

(c) Your team and look out for their well-being. Train them to think about your objective, take care of their financial needs, and discipline/reward them.

(3) **DO:**

(a) **SEEK RESPONSIBILITY and TAKE RESPONSIBILITY FOR YOUR ACTIONS:** Leaders must exercise initiative, be resourceful, and take advantage of opportunities that will lead to victory. Accept just criticism and take corrective actions for mistakes.

(b) **MAKE SOUND AND TIMELY DECISIONS:** Rapidly assess situations and make sound decisions. Gather essential information, announce decisions in time for your team to assist you, and consider short- and long-term effects of your decision.

(c) **SET THE EXAMPLE:** Be a role model for others. Set high, but attainable standards, be willing to do what you require of your team, and share dangers and hardships with your support network.

(d) **KEEP YOUR SUBORDINATES INFORMED:** Keeping your subordinates informed helps them make decisions and execute plans within your intent; it encourages initiative, improves teamwork, and enhances morale.

(e) **DEVELOP A SENSE OF RESPONSIBILITY IN SUBORDINATES:** Teach, challenge, and develop subordinates. Delegation indicates you trust your subordinates and will make them want even more responsibility.

(f) **ENSURE THE TASK IS UNDERSTOOD, SUPERVISED, AND ACCOMPLISHED:** Your team needs to now what you expect from them: What you want done, what the standard is, and when you want it.

(g) **BUILD THE TEAM:** Train and cross train your team until they are confident in the team's technical/tactical abilities. Develop a team spirit that motivates them to go willingly and to confidently approach each opportunity.

(h) **EMPLOY YOUR TEAM IN ACCORDANCE WITH ITS CAPABILITIES:** Know the capabilities and limitations of your team. As a leader you are responsible to recognize both of these factors and employ your team accordingly.

Those are the principles we have in the military. Application of those principles helped me throughout my military career as well as in the business world.

Know your allies (i.e., mentors, supportive family and friends) and know your enemies (those counter to your goals and expectations). My allies continuously provide me with emotional support and encouragement. They provide positive reinforcement and constructive feedback. They are not "yes" men or women. They act as my sounding board and enable me to objectively question my thought process. We share a great deal of respect and admiration for each other. My success is their success and vice versa. These allies have been within my family, my military commanders and peers, my West Point classmates, and my colleagues.

Wright

Are there other lessons you learned in the military that you practice in your current career? For example, I'm sure discipline was a major part of your Army career.

Scott

Discipline was a major part of my Army career, but I learned discipline before I joined the service. Fortunately I grew up in a disciplined household. Also, as an athlete, I had a chance to learn discipline early on through the competitive environment of athletics. Often we think about the military as a primary place to learn discipline but well before I got into the military I had another training ground for discipline. The military just gave me another opportunity to develop and strengthen good habits.

What discipline does is teach one to delay gratification, which has been the cornerstone of my success. It gave me the ability to be forward looking. Knowing my goal routinely enables me to step back and assess the situation ensuring I do the things most congruent with allowing me to reach my desired outcome versus getting off track because of something immediate. I learned to be more proactive than reactive and only through discipline was I able to do that.

Courage has also been a contributor to my success. Overcoming life's obstacles and making it to the top in all endeavors requires brave actions at some point, as well as the ability to conquer fears. I think that all self-made millionaires have courage because accumulating wealth often requires taking risks, including financial risks. Economic risk-taking is a requirement for becoming financially independent. The benefits of becoming financially independent are greater than the risks often associated with accumulating wealth. Believing this and taking action is courageous in and of itself. The fear of economic failure is not easy to overcome and that's why so few people have the courage to take that leap of faith into the possible.

My **faith in God** has been essential to my success throughout my life. I was deployed to fight during Operation Desert Storm at the age of nineteen. Prior to deploying, I made a video will that I sent to my family stating that I did not know if I would return. Safely returning from that experience gave me an incredible appreciation for life and all that my faith in God has meant to me. I am thankful for my life, my family, and my relationships. I vowed to live life to the fullest and attempt to realize my potential, as God would have me to do. I know that I am and have always been blessed.

Hard work, planning, decisiveness, positive thinking, mind control, and remaining physically, mentally, and emotionally fit are other variables that make up my personal success equation.

Wright

You've really done some remarkable things in the world of finance. How did you get into real estate investment? Was it something that interested you when you were growing up?

Scott

When I was in high school, I sat down one day and thought about what I wanted for my life. Actually, I prayed for direction. Early on I knew I wanted to become financially independent and I wanted to achieve wealth, not only for me, but also for my family.

Robert Allen, author of *Multiple Streams of Income,* stated that "Money, by itself, is neither good nor bad, it's neutral. Money is an energy tool. Like a hammer, money can be used to build or to destroy." I believe that understanding money, how to ethically make it, keep it, and share it, adds a positive dimension to wealth. Our lives, our relationships, and our happiness improve when there is enough money. Money properly earned and combined with enlightened intentions makes the world a better place. I didn't grow up in a household that had a lot of money or anyone I could emulate from the standpoint of financial well-being. However, I was surrounded by hard-working people. I can remember Dad saying, "Money don't grow on trees." I had a certain phobia up until the age of twenty-seven. Today, I call it "debt phobia."

With that said I did some very proactive research to identify what things could potentially help me reach my goal of financial independence. I narrowed it down to business and real estate. With that thought in mind, as I got older I worked on establishing my credit and increasing my knowledge about investing in general. I then started reading and taking the proactive steps of learning what was necessary for me to get started in the business of real estate. I received my first real estate book as a birthday gift in 1998. It was titled, *How to Buy Your Home . . . and do it right,* by Sue Beck. When I was ready, I put a contract on my first home. As Stephen Covey writes in his book *The 7 Habits of Highly Effective People,* I began with the end in mind.

Wright

I'd like to dig into your situation a little deeper, Nate. I'm sure everyone reading this book is asking the question, "Did he *really* build a net worth of over one million dollars in just fifteen months and if he did, can I do it too?" Will you tell us more about this aspect of your story?

Scott

Just for clarification, there are two key financial statements that we all should learn to understand: income statement and balance sheet. Income minus expenses equals cash flow; whereas, net worth is the difference between your assets and your liabilities.

Here's my story: I was in my last three months of military service when I realized that if I didn't take action right then it would be much more difficult for me to get financing in the immediate future because I would be in between jobs, changing careers. One question bankers typically ask is for a history of income. Knowing this would be a problem, I aggressively began looking for income producing properties to purchase. During that time I stayed true to the discipline of finding the right property in the right location for the right price.

After looking at listings for over a hundred properties, I called upon one property in particular and decided to go see it. It met my criteria and I put it under contract. Later during the week, I called on another property and realized that I had called the same phone number earlier—the owner had two different properties on the market for sale. Since I already had one of the houses under contract, I asked the seller about the second property he had listed. I looked at the second property and was able to negotiate a package deal to acquire both properties at a substantial reduction in the asking price. (This is something I always want to do—find something that I can make a good deal for.)

That one deal saved me over $125,000. The very next project I looked at, within the next thirty days of putting the first properties under contract, was a forty-unit apartment complex. That complex was located three hours away from where I was living. It was an area I had never heard of, never been to, and had no information about; but I went ahead and called on it. It interested me enough to take the drive up to the location and the numbers made sense so I ended up putting the forty-unit project under contract. Through negotiations with the seller I was able to acquire that property at a discount of over $100,000 and the seller took back a note of 15 percent of the purchase price. I only put 5 percent into the deal. The forty-unit apartment complex is where most of the cash flow came from. As a result of capital improvements, management, raising the rents, and decreasing expenses, I was able to increase the value of this income producing property. Over the fifteen months of holding them, those projects grew in value and provided the foundation for my personal net worth to grow.

Wright

Do you think real estate investing is something anyone can do? What are the risks—the downside to this kind of investing?

Scott

Anyone can be a successful real estate investor *if* they are willing to get involved and are disciplined enough to find the deal and run the numbers up front versus getting caught up in the emotions of what they think is happening—trend following. I was L-U-C-K-Y—

Labor Under Correct Knowledge. I think that one would find, through just going through the real estate section in a library or a bookstore, that individuals who have experienced success have the exact same story but it's worded differently—the principles are exactly the same. We share the exact same philosophy about doing the business. The thing about real estate is you can be a trader, you can be a growth and income person, or you can be strictly an income person. There are many ways a person can make money in real estate.

The downside is that individuals don't go in with knowledge. The knowledge doesn't have to be internal; it could be knowledge from external sources also. Individuals jump into it because they hear of the excitement and all the success stories. From an investment standpoint real estate in and of itself is no different than stocks, bonds, and securities. If you go into it with no knowledge, if you go into it haphazardly, you can lose and most likely you will lose your money. You should have an understanding of how to maximize your profits from the following:

- **Buying and holding**
- **Using other people's money (OPM) and other people's time (OPT) and other people's knowledge (OPK)**
- **Buying, fixing, and selling**
- **Quick turning, flipping, and wholesaling**
- **Lease optioning**

What I see in today's market is that many people call themselves investors but are in essence speculators. I'm particularly referring to the big craze on flipping new construction. I don't get excited about that particular vehicle—it's the objective at the end that drives whether or not I'm in real estate or something else, depending on what the overall plan is.

I would recommend that you determine whether the industry fits into your plan and that you understand the pros and the cons. Once you do that and feel comfortable with it and understand it is an active investment (it can be active or passive), you are ready to invest. If you want to have an active investment, realize that you've got to have systems in place to run it just like a business. There are enough proven systems out there so you don't have to "reinvent the wheel."

Also, there are a lot of guys like me who offer coaching services for a fee. The value we provide is that you get an expert to walk you through the deal. This is the leverage of OPK (**O**ther **P**eople's **K**nowledge). You save time and money by investing in the coaching relationship. "A thousand mile journey begins with the first step that can only be taken one step at a time." I'll help you to start living the life that you've dreamed about.

Wright

I've always wondered if some people just have a knack for making money in real estate or the stock market, for example, and others couldn't make a profit if their lives depended on it. Do you see it that way?

Scott

The people who may be seen as having a "knack" for being successful are people who have done the work at the front side of their success. In other words, they prepared for their success. They worked to reach their success—they've made their own luck.

I just finished reading a book about the difference between a job and work. The difference is a job is something you get paid for. Work is something you do independent of getting paid. A great athlete or a doctor will put in work well before the time they earned the designation of professional and the ensuing big paycheck. Likewise, most people who are successful in investing in general have done the work up front. They just make it look easy because what is seen is the end result. The effort that went into preparing for their opportunity is not as visible. For example, when Magic Johnson was at the top of his game that's all we saw and all that we expected. The dedication, commitment, and drive he had to succeed were not as visible as his success. The same holds true for him today in business. I guess you can say that Magic has been "lucky" too.

Wright

What an interesting conversation. It's so important to have money and to be independently wealthy because everybody's living longer now and things are happening to people. Being financially secure is on the minds of all American people, at least that's true for the ones I know.

I really appreciate your taking all this time with me Nate, to answer all these financial questions and telling us a little bit about your story. I've learned a lot and I'm sure that people who read this book will.

Today we've been talking with Nathaniel Scott, Jr. He built a net worth of over a million dollars on a very modest income with a $10,000 a month positive cash flow and he did it in just over fifteen months. Today, he owns over five million dollars in real estate properties. He is the president of DNA Business Services, which is a private consulting business offering Executive Coaching and Personal CFO services. In addition to church and family commitments, he serves as board president of Rebuilding Together Northeast Florida, a nonprofit organization whose mission is to preserve and revitalize houses and communities, assuring that low-income homeowners—particularly those who are elderly, disabled, or families with children—live in comfort, safety, and independence. He's doing exactly what he intended to do, as he said—he's working his plan which must include working for the betterment of people around him.

Nate, thank you so much for being with us today on *Pillars of Success*.

About the Author

NATHANIEL SCOTT, JR., MBA, RFC, is a former enlisted soldier, war veteran, West Point Cadet, Army Ranger, and U.S. Army Captain. He applied the same level of focus and discipline that he displayed in the military to actively pursue his interests in business and real estate. The end result was the acquisition of over a million dollars in assets in ninety days, generating $10,000 in monthly cash flow and financial independence at thirty-three.

Nathaniel Scott, Jr., MBA, RFC

DNA Business Services, LLC

14477 Lake Jessup Drive

Jacksonville, FL 32258

Phone: 904.838.2623

E-mail: Nscott1996@comcast.net

www.DNABusinessServices.com

Chapter Ten

WILL KEIM, PH.D.

David E. Wright (Wright)

Today we're speaking with Dr. Will Keim who has spoken to over two million people from two thousand collegiate and corporate campuses in every state in the United States. He holds a Ph.D. from Oregon State University and is a Paul Harris Fellow for Rotary International. His corporate clients included Bushnell, Swiss Army, Luxottica, Lenscrafters, Eye Med, AT&T, IBM, State Farm Insurance, and the Children's Miracle Network. Dr. Keim was awarded the prestigious Jack Anson Award for Outstanding Interfraternalism in 2001 from the Association of Fraternity Advisors. He is a National Collegiate Athletic Association Recognized Speaker on CHAMPS Life Skills and Alcohol and Drug Issues. Dr. Keim received his BA and MA in Speech Communication and Religious Studies from the University of the Pacific where he was a four-year Division I letterman in baseball. He is the author of seven books and a contributing author to several other books including *Let Your Leadership Speak,* and *Chicken Soup for the College Soul.* He is the father of four wonderful children, ages nineteen, fifteen, twelve/twelve (twins), and the husband for twenty-six years to Donna Keim.

Thank you so much, Dr. Keim, for being with us on *Pillars of Success*.

Dr. Will Keim (Keim)

It's nice to be with you.

David Wright (Wright)

You have traveled widely and spoken to millions of people about success. How do you think our culture defines success?

Keim

I think that's part of the problem—our culture tends to define success in terms of the amount of money you have or the amount of possessions in your control. That creates a real sense of urgency for people to go out and make a lot of money and buy a lot of things and get into a lot of debt. The problem with that definition of success is that you can never have as much money as you think you need or desire and you can never have the newest and most updated "toys." It's a description of success that, by its own definition, is self-defeating and can never be achieved. This is why I believe so many people do not feel successful.

The best definition of success that has been written is by John Wooden who coached at UCLA for twenty-seven seasons and all twenty-seven were winning seasons. He won nineteen Conference championships, ten national championships—seven of them in a row and four with undefeated seasons. More importantly, he graduated 98.75 percent of his players. In 1957 he took two African American players to a post-season tournament and when told to, "Take the Negro boys home," informed the tournament committee that he didn't see color—he saw effort—and if *all* his players weren't welcome, *none* of them were. He pulled his team out of the tournament and in effect, changed the way we play sports in this country.

John Wooden, Purdue University graduate, said the following, "Success is the peace of mind that comes from knowing you did the best you were capable of doing and you're the only one who will ever know that."

He built a pyramid of success, which is a wonderful thing for people in the corporate world, or students, or anyone looking for a model of success. It basically comes from each person looking in the mirror and knowing they did their very best and then having the peace of mind that comes from that because, in reality, you can fool all the people all the time but the one person you can't fool is the person looking back at you in the mirror. Wooden wanted people to be focused on doing their best whether they were teaching, or preaching, in real estate, or in sports, or in business—to do their best and they would ultimately achieve peace of mind; ergo, success from that.

Wright

Are these success characteristics—are there common character traits that successful people have and act on?

Keim

I think there are many traits and characteristics but there are ten that are most important. Those characteristics include:

Listening—The ability to listen not only to other people but to listen to your internal voice. If people are spiritual it could be called listening to the spirit. If people are secular it could be called the conscience. Everybody has a voice inside that tells them whether they're doing the right thing or the wrong thing.

Empathy—This is the ability to put yourself in someone else's position. Native Americans have long been given credit for the saying, "Never criticize a man until you've walked a mile in his moccasins." That means don't judge someone. Empathy is the ability to put yourself in someone else's position, to feel their pain.

Action—The ability to not be a reactor—to wait for things to happen—but to step up and create action. In his recent book on leadership, Tom Peters said that leaders not only have to act outside the box, they have to build a new box. They have to create something that's never existed before and I call that "action" rather than reaction.

Delegation—People who are successful know how to get quality help from other successful people. We have a myth in our culture where someone can be a "self-made man" or a "self-made woman" and there is no such thing. People need other people in order to be successful. Truly successful people know that. Bill Gates is an example of someone who built a tremendous organization of people he trusts and empowers, people who tell him the truth, and people he relies on for expertise in areas that he doesn't have expertise in. Truly successful people can delegate and receive help and criticism from other people.

Enthusiasm—Successful people are almost uniformly enthusiastic about what they do, who they are, and more importantly who they surround themselves with. Successful people are magnets for people who are enthusiastic and who listen or who are empathic, active, and people who are helpful and delegate authority. They are always positive and upbeat. Very few successful people are "downers." Very few successful people drag everyone down with them; instead they lift everyone.

Reflection—Successful people take time daily to reflect. I call this the hour of power where first, they take thirty minutes a day in prayer, meditation, or contemplation. After that they go out and exercise their bodies—to do something physical. You can do curls at a bar, lifting a sixteen-ounce glass of beer or you can do curls in the gym— one of these activities is going to be more productive than the other. People who can take an hour a day to exercise their body and exercise their sense of contemplation; people who revitalize their sense of awe and wonder are people we call "re-creators"—people of reflection.

Stewardship—Successful people understand that they are caretakers of resources and places and positions. They don't own everything that is in their life—they realize they are on the planet to serve, they've been given an opportunity to steward these resources and every successful person, when they leave an organization, a campus, or an office building, their goal is that when they're gone, the organization is stronger, therefore they steward and they mentor and they take care of the protégés—the people who work with and for them. They're not the kind of people who, when they leave an organization say, "Boy, they're going to miss me when I'm gone. This place will fall flat on its face." Those aren't successful people. Successful people steward and build something greater and larger than themselves.

Humor—Successful people can laugh at themselves. They know that if they don't learn to laugh at themselves other people will do it for them, so successful people laugh and smile and they find the humor in things. One of the most successful, well-known writers in American history and in the world, Mark Twain, once wrote a book titled, *Quarrels with Heaven*, in which he said if he were God there are a few things he would do differently, starting with the seed in an avocado—it's much too big. We need more fruit in the avocado and less seed. Obviously he was a guy with a great sense of humor that drew people to himself. Successful people don't laugh *at* people but they certainly laugh *with* other people and at themselves.

Integrity—Successful people say what they mean and do what they say and when they don't, they admit it. Successful people don't spin, they don't tell half-truths, they don't tell one group of people one thing and another group of people another thing. Successful people are men and women of integrity, who live ethically, and who say what they mean, do what they say, and are willing to stand in front of a group, or another person, or someone they're in a relationship with and say, "I screwed up. I'm sorry. Let's start over."

Patience—Successful people are patient with themselves and with others. They understand the dichotomy that many people who aren't successful want to be evaluated on their intent but they evaluate everyone else on their actions. People who aren't successful want everyone else to get what they have coming to them but they want a better deal than they have coming to them. Successful people understand that they need to be patient with themselves and patient with others because we are in a never-ending process of evolving and growing and learning. Most great teachers, most great doctors, most great statesmen and stateswomen—successful people—are patient and give people and things time.

Wright

What role does ethical decision-making have in the lives of successful people?

Keim

Especially these days with media attention, and the advent of the Internet, you can't do anything without someone noticing. Successful people make ethical decisions. There's a very simple model on how to do that created by Dr. J. Wesley Robb at the University of Southern California. I spoke at a conference with him a number of years ago. He was retiring right after the conference. He gave this model and I went up to him afterwards and said it was brilliant. He told me, "It's yours, take it." I said, "It's about ethics—I'm going to give you credit for it. I'm not going to pretend it's mine." The model is very simple and it says this:

Before anyone acts, before anything is done, four questions need to be answered:

1. Why am I doing this? What is my intent?
2. Is it legal? Is it according to policy?
3. What are the consequences of this behavior or action?
4. How does what I'm about to do fit in with my moral principles? Is this consistent with what I see myself to be?

Successful people very simply behave in total concert with their ethical framework and their moral principles. Their deeds follow their words. In this day and age it's a very rare thing but it will truly mark the successful people of the twenty-first century.

Wright

It would seem that conflict is inevitable in our corporate, collegiate, and community life together. Is there a way to resolve conflict peacefully to increase the likelihood of success?

Keim

Absolutely. Whenever people get together there's going to be conflict. We call conflict within an individual the field of psychology. We call conflict between groups sociology. We call conflict between cultures anthropology. The history of the world is the history of conflict. It's not that we can avoid conflict, it's what do we do when it surfaces. I think there are five things successful people can do:

1. Specificity—When successful people confront one another they are specific about things they are disagreeing about. My parents, God rest their souls, argued about two or three things over dinner on most nights—they weren't even on the same page. Consequently, when they weren't specific they never reached a resolution of their problems. Successful people are specific about the things they disagree about.
2. Don't moralize—Successful people don't turn everything into a "you either agree with me or burn in hell" scenario. We have become so polemic in our society—you're either with us or against us. I'm seeking the high middle ground that Senator Mark Hatfield of the great state of Oregon used to stand on when he considered issues. The high ground isn't on one side of the fence or on the other but tries to find some dry land in the middle of an issue where discussion can begin.
3. Talk one-to-one—Successful people don't practice "drive-by insults" in newspapers or on e-mail. E-mail is a very powerful thing but in the old days, when you wanted to insult someone you had to write a letter and put a stamp on it. Usually, on the way to the mailbox, you reconsider and rewrite the letter. Now, when you hit "send" your insult is instantaneous. We

need people to talk one-to-one, face-to-face if they want to resolve conflict.

4. Be rested and not stressed—Successful people resolve conflict when they're not stressed out, when they're not tired, and in our culture, when they've not had a three-martini lunch. We need people to deal with issues in a sober and non-stress situation.

5. Always leave the door open—We slam a lot of doors in people's faces electronically these days with things we wish we hadn't said. We need to leave the door open and agree to disagree and to agree to take a time out. We need to say, "You are of this opinion and I'm of another. Let's give this a little bit of time and we'll get back and discuss it again." That way you can resolve conflict interpersonally and peacefully.

Wright

Will you talk to our readers a little more about John Wooden and why he has had such an impact on your life and your understanding of success?

Keim

When I was a high school student in Southern California, Pacific Gas and Electric gave each high school student a card with Coach Wooden's picture on it and the pyramid of success and the definition of success. We all watched him on television coach UCLA and all the great teams he coached there. I actually went home early from my prom once because the taped delay of the UCLA game was going to be on. (I don't think I dated that young woman again, by her choice, but at least I got to see UCLA beat USC.)

Wooden is a man whose words and deeds were totally consistent. He coached and he was married to his lovely wife for fifty-three years until she passed away in 1994. During every game he coached he'd turn around and give her the thumbs up sign. In his left hand he carried a cross that he'd been given in World War II from his chaplain when they went into battle. He hid the cross with a program because he thought faith was such a private matter it shouldn't be worn in public. Nobody asked the coach about a rolled up program in his left hand but under the program was a cross because the chaplain told him it would get him home to see his lovely wife, Nell.

To this day John meets with the UCLA Women's Gymnastics Team once or twice a month and talks to them about character and values and ethics. The man is over ninety years old and he can still speak to eighteen- nineteen- or twenty-year-old college students. This is because the ethics he teaches are timeless: his word is his bond and his word is his deed.

Throughout my high school life I waited for a call from Coach Wooden because I knew he was looking for a six-foot-one, 160-pound center. It never came but nonetheless I've been able to exchange some letters and contact through other coaches, to try and share with this man the deep impact he had on people. I hope he lives another fifty years; but when Coach Wooden goes there will be a public display of affection that is normally reserved for heads of state and Nobel Prize winners. He's a gracious, kind, loving man who cared about his students and is a role model for anyone who wants to be successful. When I talk to any young person who says they want to be a success, I tell them to read the book, *They Call Me Coach,* by John Wooden and they'll know exactly what they need to do and how to become the man or woman they need to be because he lived it out in his life.

He's a legend, he's in the coaching and playing Hall of Fame, and more importantly, he's just the kind of man thousands of people have gone to and never once has he chosen not to mentor those people. He's a great, great American.

Wright

When Pat Summit from my university (University of Tennessee) broke Coach Wooden's winning record last year, Coach Wooden was the first person to say kind words about it.

Keim

It was interesting too because somebody asked him about Coach Pat. I've worked with her team—with Chamique Holdsclaw and Semeka Randall—and had wonderful discussions with her and Mickie DeMoss (Mickie was her assistant then and is now head coach at Kentucky). Coach Wooden said, "She [Coach Pat] would have won those games had she coached men!" I thought, "What a great thing to say because: (a) it's true, but (b) nobody would be happier for her than he was because he understands what it takes to get the best out of young people.

Wright

Who are some other successful people you have met in your travels and what makes them successful?

Keim

I've been in every state in the U.S. at least five times and I've been in every city with more than a population of 100,000 over the last twenty years; it's just crazy.

There are some people who really stand out. One of them is Lou Holtz, former head football coach of the University of South Carolina and Notre Dame. I met Coach Holtz in Atlanta in Delta's Crown Room Club a long, long time ago. I said to him, "I'm at a point in my career where I could really use someone famous saying something nice about me. We're in the same fraternity."

He gave me the handshake and then he said, "Send me a tape of what you do and I'll take a look at it." One week later he sent a note out which is on all of my promotional materials. It opened the doors of the NCAA to me. He included a note with the comment saying, "I love what you do and your message is totally consistent with my message. But even if I hadn't liked it as much as I do, I would have said something good about you because when a brother asks another brother for help, it's that brother's moral responsibility to help him."

I thought I'm some Podunk guy from Oregon (at that point I think I was in my late twenties). He had no reason to help me—there's nothing in it for him but he stepped forward and helped me in a way that was just outstanding.

Another guy I've met along the way whom I really enjoyed was H. Ross Perot. He and I were keynote speakers at the U.S. Air Force Academy Symposium on Character and Leadership. Mr. Perot walked into the room and of course was a magnet for anyone who was important—the commandants of all the service academies, the corporate leaders who were there, and the senators—but Mr. Perot took time in that room to talk with every single person he did not know. He doesn't need to advance his career by talking to Dr. Will Keim from Corvallis, Oregon; but he took time, was interested, and is the kind of man who will look you straight in the eye, not over your shoulder to see if there is someone more important coming next. He is just a fabulous human being.

I also had the opportunity when in Atlanta at one point to see Coretta Scott King. She showed she had the same gift that Ross Perot has—to look each person in the eye with the keen ability to make you feel as if perhaps what you said to her next was going to be the most important thing that she heard. She doesn't look over your shoulder looking to see who's next, and doesn't dismiss people. I like to call that "presence."

Perhaps that's a great tip about success—the ability to be present in each and every situation with each and every person you meet, in case that person needs something from you or has something to offer, you're fully there to receive it. I think that's a good success tip in business. I think it's great in education and I know it's important in parenting and building a family life—just to be present.

One of the most amazing people I had the pleasure of meeting was Coach Pat Summitt of the University of Tennessee. I spoke to her basketball team when she was in the process of winning, I believe, her third straight championship. She had All-American Chamique Holdsclaw on the team, as well as Semeka Randall, Kellie (Jolly) Harper, and many great players. They were all sitting in the front row. Peyton Manning and the football team were right behind them.

Just before my speech I asked Semeka, "Why are y'all sitting in the very front row?"

"Because Coach Pat tells us to sit in the front of the lectures, in the front of our classes, and in the front of the buses so we get used to being in front of things like the SEC and the NCAA," she replied.

Six national titles and nine hundred wins are hard to argue with!

That story stuck with me because excellence comes from practicing it in your daily life, not when it is convenient or every once in awhile. I learned something that day from Coach Pat and her players that I never forgot. I have passed that on to my children and when Tennessee came out West to play the University of Portland, my girls got to meet Coach Pat and her players. Six girls came out of the locker room walking tall with their shoulders back and proud. It touched my family and me very much.

Wright

What do you consider your greatest accomplishments, your greatest successes? What obstacles or barriers have you overcome to reach them?

Keim

I never used to talk very publicly about my barriers and obstacles because I thought at the time everybody had their own issues and their own burdens and carry. But I had a student come up to me after an address who said, "I really appreciate your talk on success and leadership; but it's easy for you, you have a Ph.D. and four kids and everything is great in your life." I realized I had inadvertently and accidentally portrayed that through my introduction and my speaking.

I said, "Well, son, I have to tell you my real dad passed away three months before I was born. My stepfather was a great dad but he was an alcoholic. When I was eight years old I was sexually molested. So I've had some obstacles and barriers to overcome too. He immediately bonded with me. I include a short segment in my speeches and presentations now about my obstacles.

What this taught me was I don't need to appear as some guy who says, "All you need to do to have a successful life is to be like me." I don't want my students and my interns to be like me, I want them to be like themselves, so I share those obstacles only to let them know that I know they've had some obstacles and hurdles too but that together we can get over those. With help we can get over those, with good friends, and with surrounding ourselves with successful people we play through these tough things.

My greatest accomplishments are very simple. With all the things I've done and the awards I've won, the only thing that really, really matters to me is that I have four great children. It's not bragging, David, if it's true. They are positive and they are helpful.

One of my friends, Dr. Michael Anthony Ingram, came to my home. He's a poet and a PhD in Educational Counseling. He came over to have dinner and when I walked out to the car with him he said, "Will, I don't think your children know that I'm black."

I said, "Michael, I don't know how they'd miss that because you are black."

"What I'm trying to say to you," he said, "is I think your children treated me tonight like I was a performance poet and a professor at the university."

That's the kind of feedback I get from people when they come to my house. My kids volunteer at shelters. They walk down the streets of our town to say hello to homeless guys and call them by name because they know them.

I've done some things that haven't turned out great in my life but the thing I've done in concert with my wife is we have four wonderful children who are going to "put a dent in the world" to use the language Tom Peters uses. They're going to make a dent—they're going to make the world a better place.

Wright

You have spoken to more young adults about success, character, leadership, and ethics than anyone in our society. What is the key teaching in your presentations?

Keim

Whether this is in a corporate meeting with a bunch of people in suits or it's to students dressed in a manner that quite frankly I'm not sure I understand, the key teaching in life is to never, ever give up. Jim Valvano said that when he was dying of cancer. It became a phrase for the Jimmy V Foundation. I teach them to never, ever give up on themselves, on their parents, on life, on their country; to never, ever give up and, in the process of that, to say what they mean and do what they say and when they don't, admit it.

We're in such a time of spin and incomplete sentences and people practicing phraseology when a little truth and honesty would be better. Mark Twain said, "Always tell the truth, it will amaze half the people and astonish the rest." I'm a big believer in never giving up on yourself and to really say what you mean and do what you say and admit your mistakes because I've found that with honesty, most people are very forgiving and they'll give you a second chance. I think we're in a world that is growing tired of spin and tired of schemes— they want the truth. It's a rare commodity and I urge my audiences to tell it and to live it.

Wright

Is there one thing *every* successful person must understand *every* day in every situation?

Keim

There is one thing I think of every single day when my eyes first open. I'm always thankful that I get another chance to be the man, the husband, the father, the teacher I've always wanted to be—every day gives me a chance to move closer to that. We, in our culture, do everything we can to put off death, at times by trying to make ourselves look younger with age defying cream for our eyes. Sometimes we send our older people away so we don't have to acknowledge the fact that we're getting old too.

Every single day I think of the number 25,000. That is the number of days you get when you're born—maybe more with good health and exercise or maybe less with inherited genetic diseases, but the fact is that it's about 25,000. I'm fifty years old and that means I've had 15,000 of my 25,000 days. I have 10,000 days left, so I don't really have time to waste. Even a college student has 18,500 days left. If you're older—if you're in your sixties or seventies, well, you do the math.

We need to get up every day and we need to get busy because life is not a dress rehearsal. This is not a warm-up act for something else. Life is a one-ticket ride. We're working without a net and we need to get busy. Every day when I wake up I say, "Ah, what am I going to exchange for this twenty-four-hour period I've found myself living in?" I think every successful person has the same sense of urgency I have that is caused by the humility of knowing Bill Gates and I live in two different worlds and Nelson Mandela and I live in two different worlds and Bishop Tutu lives in a different world, and when she was alive Indira Gandhi lived in a different world than I do. But the one thing we all have in common is we're all in the process of checking out. Successful people know therefore that they can't waste time. They don't put things off. They don't plan to say tomorrow what could be said today or do tomorrow what could be done today. They get up every day and they do exactly what needs to be done today and they don't take tomorrow for granted. That to me is the key thing successful people know. Successful people are urgent, they are focused on today, and tomorrow will be good because they're going to make today a quality day. They build a lifetime of those sequential things based on that understanding that life is short and we need to get busy.

Wright

What an interesting conversation. I have learned a lot here today and I'm sure our readers will. I really appreciate your taking so much time to talk with us today.

Keim

Thank you very much, David. I appreciate your calling and I wish you continued success.

Wright

Today we've been talking with Dr. Will Keim who has spoken to over two million people from two thousand collegiate and corporate campuses in every state in the nation. He's the author of seven books and contributing author to several other books including, *Let Your Leadership Speak* and *Chicken Soup for the College Soul*. His greatest accomplishment, however, in his own words is that he is the father of four wonderful children.

Thank you so much, Dr. Keim, for being with us today on *Pillars of Success*.

About The Author

DR. WILL KEIM has spoken personally to over two million people from two thousand collegiate and corporate campuses. His corporate clients include Luxottica, Eye Med, Lenscrafters, AT&T, IBM, The Ford Foundation, OACP, Bushnell, State Farm Insurance, and Swiss Army. He is a Paul Harris Fellow from Rotary International and holds the Jack Anson Award from the Association of Fraternity Advisors. He is the International Chaplain for Delta Upsilon Fraternity and an Intercollegiate Chaplain for The Christian Church (Disciples of Christ). Dr. Keim was selected as the Outstanding Professor at Oregon State University during his teaching there and was chosen as an Outstanding Young Man of America by the U.S. Jaycees. He is a National Collegiate Athletic Association (NCAA) recognized Speaker on Life Skills and Substance Abuse Issues, and has spoken in every state in the United States at least three times. Dr. Keim keynoted the United States Air Force Academy National Symposium on Character and Leadership with Mr. Ross Perot who said of his work, "When Dr. Keim speaks, I would advise you to listen and then live the principles he is teaching with passion and purpose." He is married and the father of four wonderful children. Dr. Keim is an avid fisherman and gardener, and the author of six books.

Will Keim, Ph.D.
Phone: 800.848.3897
E-mail: willkeim@willkeim.com
www.willkeim.com

Chapter Eleven

PAT SUMMITT

David E. Wright (Wright)

We're talking today with Pat Summitt who is a living legend at the University of Tennessee. As coach of the University of Tennessee Lady Volunteers, she has led her team to six NCAA titles. In 1997–1998 the Lady Vols finished 39–0 and won a third consecutive NCAA title. The Lady Vols have played in more than forty states, five foreign countries and in every imaginable venue. Pat is also a player personnel consultant for the WNBA's Washington Mystics.

She became the Tennessee coach at age twenty-two and before that she played on the 1976 U.S. Olympic silver medal basketball team. In 1984 she coached the American women to the first gold medal in their history. Pat is considered by many to be the best women's basketball coach in the history of the game.

Pat Summitt, welcome to *Pillars of Success!*

Pat Summitt (Summitt)

Thank you. It's great to be here.

Wright

In 1997 you were recognized as one of the twenty-five most influential working mothers by *Working Mother* magazine. What kind of impact has raising a family had on your professional life?

Summitt

I think it's probably been a greater challenge personally, as far as trying to balance everything; but clearly I think having a son has taught me an awful lot about working with young people. It's much like coaching. It's teaching every day, teaching life skills, the responsibility for young people, be it shortly after they're born to seventeen-year-olds. I think there's been a lot of carryover from being a mom to being a coach.

Wright

How old is he now?

Summitt

He's fourteen.

Wright

I got to meet him. He hangs out with all the girls, doesn't he?

Summitt

He does; he really enjoys that.

Wright

Pat, your athletes tell us you are the perfect role model and that you instill a desire to be successful by challenging them to reach their potential, both on and off the court. Tell us about some of your successful graduates.

Summitt

When you've been coaching as long as I have obviously you have a lot of people who are out there working professionally, whether it's in sales or another area. We have young ladies with Coca-Cola, we have people in marketing and one young lady is in New York working for the Big Apple Circus; she is a key marketer for that event. We have a couple here in Knoxville right now in real estate. We've had a doctor, nurse, interior decorator—it's a variety. A lot of our recent graduates have gone into the professional league and are playing for the WNBA.

We're a pretty diverse group and I think the important thing is that they have all left here with diplomas. They have all left here and been able to go on and pursue their dreams or their careers. A lot of them are moms. Unfortunately, a lot more of them had little boys than little girls. When I start coaching the players' daughters I think it may be time to hang it all up. What do you think?

Wright

You could be right.

You're the first female coach to be featured on the cover of *Sports Illustrated*. How did that make you feel?

Summitt

After I got past the picture I felt pretty good. The photograph on the cover was not exactly the most flattering picture, but I don't think they were looking for that to begin with. I think most people want to look at the intensity of my style and that's fine, because I'm proud of the fact that we work hard here and we're very intense when we're on the court. Certainly to be the first female coach featured in that regard was a tremendous honor and a great compliment.

Wright

Do you think it advanced the cause of women in sports and women coaches?

Summitt

I think that a number of things have allowed us to improve the image of our program, and the growth of our sport has benefited from it, be it things like *Sports Illustrated* or in particular now, national television exposure. I know our HBO documentary touched a lot of young kids back in the 1997 season. It was a documentary that let young people know it's not easy. Athletics is a lot like life. It's challenging and you go through some adverse times and if you're persistent and you work through them in the right fashion, and with a team, you have a chance to be successful in whatever you do.

Wright

Pat, you're the author of two bestsellers: *Reach for the Summit* and *Raise the Roof*. You talk a lot about the influence of your father in your first book. Will you tell us a little bit about your father?

Summitt

Alexandria, he's certainly a stern, strong individual, which was good for me and for the five kids. He was a confident man, very committed to working hard. He wanted us at a very young age to learn responsibility and work ethic and not to be afraid of hard work and not to be afraid to compete. It's had a significant impact on my life. First of all, I didn't mind rolling up my sleeves and doing whatever I was asked to do. No job was too big or too small. I knew that if I worked hard enough I could be successful. Certainly that has really stuck with me. It's something I don't think I'll ever lose.

Wright

Pat, will you tell our audience where they can get copies of *Reach for the Summit* or *Raise the Roof?*

Summitt

I know that right now both are only available in paperback. I think they can be found at most of the big bookstores in any major city.

Wright

Let me change the subject for a minute. The purpose of this program is to help people be better and to live more fulfilled lives. We hope that the examples of our successful guests will help them in this goal. In this connection, has adversity played an important part in your life and career?

Summitt

Certainly it has. In particular when I tore my ACL—anterior cruciate ligament, the ligament in my left knee—when I was a senior in college. It was the first time that basketball was taken away from me. I think as kids and young people we sometimes think we have the world by the tail. All of a sudden I didn't have something that really made me smile and made me happy every day. When that happens, I think through adversity we really look to see who we are.

When I started to look at myself I realized that I needed to be able to handle the situation I was in. It made me more serious about my academics because I knew basketball was just a game. I had to get ready for a bigger game—the game of life. So I started to do some self-evaluation. That's when I went on and got my master's at Tennessee in a matter of one year, and I got very serious about being a professional at that particular time.

I would tell people that the world we live in is very, very challenging and there are a lot of changes; but our attitude will have an awful lot to do with how successful we are and how happy we are on a day-to-day basis. I try to never let anything break my spirit. Things might get you down, but you don't want to allow them to keep you down.

Wright

Didn't one of your stars suffer the same injury in 2001?

Summitt

Yes. In January 2001 Tamika Catchings went down with an ACL injury. She was the number one player in the country and obviously a key to what we were doing on the basketball court. That was a setback for her. It was interesting to watch her through this process because she too has had to learn to go in and focus on her rehabilitation and what she needed to do. We want to just get back up and play and say everything's going to be okay, but many times when that happens, whether it's an injury of this kind, or a sickness, or accident off the athletic field or court, we have to be able to handle it. We're better because of it, if we can get through it with the right attitude and the right commitment.

Wright

She is currently forward for the WNBA's Indiana Fever. According to a June 2005 *USA Today* report, she was diagnosed with asthma when she was in grade school and used an inhaler for a while but discarded it. En route to helping the U.S. women to gold at the 2004 Olympics, she was re-diagnosed with asthma. She uses an inhaler before games these days.

Summitt

She has worked out with our team when she was in town.

Wright

Pat, you certainly have a lot of fans. I was at my health club one day and there was a little girl working out next to me. I asked her what she did and she said, "I'm going to school because I'm going to be just like Pat Summitt. I don't know if you know who that is." She had no idea what I did or that I was getting ready to interview you, but I thought that was really great.

Pat, how has faith played a role in your life?

Summitt

I think without it we're lost. Certainly with my faith through hard times I've been able to be comfortable, grounded, and secure in my abilities and my strengths from within. I think that if you don't have it—if you're not connected—it's like being lost. Where do you turn? For me, again, I go back to my parents and I thank them for the type of upbringing and teaching we had and the fact that I grew up in a Christian environment. It certainly allowed me to be able to find myself and find where I belonged and understand faith and how important it is in every aspect of one's life.

Wright

Pat, has recruiting changed much since you began coaching? Do female students have the same basic motivations as males when you recruit them?

Summitt

I think recruiting has changed significantly. It's far more competitive, but there are many more choices. Our talent pool has grown significantly in number. I think it's individual. I don't think it's a gender issue so much as it is just how many individuals out there—be it males or females—are really motivated to go to the next level and get better. Certainly male athletes have the motivation of the NBA. While we have the WNBA, the salaries are significantly different; yet I do think, for the most part, we're seeing young women now really aspiring to come in and become better and improve their game, and that's exactly what you want.

Wright

Do almost all of the girls you recruit have as their goals to get into the professionals?

Summitt

I would say probably nine out of every ten, yes.

Wright

Do the alumni and former student athletes play an important role in recruiting, or does your success down through the years seem to draw the players?

Summitt

The NCAA doesn't allow alumni in the recruiting process. I think that's a good rule. What we sell at Tennessee, and what I think has really allowed us to generate a lot of consistency and success in recruiting, has been our graduation rate of 100 percent, our six national championships, and our sixteen Final Four appearances. I think student athletes come in here not only trying to improve their own game, but to have a chance to play for a national championship, or at least feel like they can get to a Final Four.

Wright

Is there a sense in which you can also spot future coaches?

Summitt

It's probably not as apparent as you might think. I coached Kellie Jolly, a great point guard out of Sparta, Tennessee, who played for White County. I knew Kellie would make a great coach, but her dad was a coach—she'd been around basketball all of her life. It was real obvious to me that if she wanted to go into coaching she'd be really, really good. Jody Adams was another one I thought just really loved the game, wanted to stay with the game, and understood the game. Occasionally you'll have a player like a Jody or like a Kellie and when you have that you know it. A lot of the student athletes I've coached have gone into coaching and it's been a bit of a surprise.

Wright

How do you prepare your team for upcoming games?

Summitt

You prepare every day in practice. I think a lot of kids will say they're a gamer. That's great, but people have to understand that you must have the discipline and the will every day to prepare to get better. We talk at Tennessee about daily improvement—understanding what they can take from practice as opposed to just going through the motions or dreading going through them. If they see it as a classroom setting I think it allows them, without question, to become prepared mentally, physically, and emotionally for the game.

Wright

Do we have a system in the state of Tennessee where the girls can really learn at younger ages, almost like a farm team system?

Summitt

We have a lot of AAU teams—summer teams from ages nine or ten years old up through eighteen years old. It allows them to play in the off-season. So many times I tell our student athletes that's where you get better. The young kids in our state have had an opportunity to be involved in AAU teams and compete in the summer months. To me, that's a way you get better, just like going to summer camps. Certainly there's no substitute for working on your own game every day. If kids are willing to work on their skills it will certainly improve their game in the off-season.

Wright

I remember a few years ago when the men dominated the Olympics. They showed up on talk shows on television. I can remember almost to the man, they said the most exciting thing about the Olympics was the practice—playing each other. Is that what you're talking about with getting better?

Summitt

Definitely. I think that's a great example of how you can get better. You've got to want to get better at anything you do. So many people want to be good but they don't want to pay the price to be that good.

Wright

That's probably true in life too, isn't it?

Summitt

Without question. I see so many people in life who underachieve. We only have one life to live and we don't know if tomorrow will be here. So we have to make the most of every day. I think it's so important for people to realize that you can be whatever you want to be. You can overcome a lot of obstacles if you have the right attitude and the level of commitment necessary, and if you surround yourself with great people.

Wright

This is kind of a crazy question, Pat. Do you think your son will grow up to be a basketball player or coach?

Summitt

I'm glad you asked that. I don't know. I think he was average in terms of athletic ability in 2002, but he developed some of these skills because he came in every morning and showed me he was brushing his teeth with his left hand and he was carrying his books with his left hand. He was trying to develop that weak hand.

Wright

At the time you won your 1976 silver medal at the Olympics, did the thought of going into coaching ever enter your mind?

Summitt

Actually, David, I was coaching here.

Wright

Is that right?

Summitt

I was. I started here in 1974 and I played in the Pan Am games in the summer of 1975 and in the Olympics the summer of 1976. I was right where I wanted to be and it helped me to be going from playing to coaching at Tennessee to going and playing internationally. I think I was much more appreciative of all the roles that players play and everything that goes into developing a successful team.

Wright

I remember there was just something magical about going into the arena there at basketball time. I have a son who's in his forties now and when he was somewhere between ten and fourteen he played for the Little Big Orange—the trick ball handlers. A fellow named Gerald Oliver was the coach of the little fellows at that time. It was awesome, just walking in there. All of the basketball players, both the men and the women, kind of hovered around those little guys. I can remember a fellow—I think his name was Johnny Darden—was teaching my son how to dribble with his left hand. It was like there was no age difference. They just really loved the game.

Summitt

It's good that you have that type of exposure. The players who are playing at the collegiate level are potentially such great role models that you want them to reach out and help others.

Wright

Pat, when you retire what is the one thing you would like to have remembered from your career?

Summitt

I think the one thing would be that I made a difference for young women, whether it was through the daily teaching or relationships. Basically I want to somehow, in some small way, have a positive impact on all of the young people I've been fortunate enough to work with.

Wright

Of all the people that I've talked with, I don't think you're going to have any problem with a legacy. This has been the fastest half hour I believe I've ever experienced in my life.

We have been talking today with Pat Summitt who is coach of the University of Tennessee Lady Vols basketball team. She has led her team to six NCAA titles and is a fine, fine person. Alex and I really appreciate your taking this time with us today.

Summitt

I've thoroughly enjoyed it. I really appreciate your having me and wish you two the very best.

About The Author

No other basketball coach in the country, male or female, has enjoyed the success of Pat Head Summitt. As a player, Summitt won an Olympic silver medal in 1976, and as an international coach, she brought home the first women's basketball gold medal in Olympic competition. She led her Tennessee Lady Volunteers to six NCAA Championships and has amassed an astounding 759 career wins. On January 14, 2003, she became the first woman to reach the 800-win plateau. On March 22, 2005, she became number one on the Division I all-time wins list, surpassing Dean Smith's record of 879 wins. She is also a player personnel consultant for the WNBA's Washington Mystics. Pat Head Summitt is a proven winner, champion, master motivator, and role model.

Pat Summitt

117 Stokely Athletics Center

University of Tennessee

Knoxville, TN 37996

Phone: 865.974.4275

www.utladyvols.ocsn.com

Chapter Twelve

RUSS ROGERS

David E. Wright (Wright)

Today we're talking with Russ Rogers. Russ is a proven leader in the business world and devoted to helping other companies succeed through his leadership, communication, and teamwork training. Russ is a member of The National Speakers Association and has enjoyed speaking to major companies such as: Honda, Asbury, Eastman Chemicals, DTS, CC Holmes, NADA 20 Groups and many others. Russ will keep you captivated whether you hear him as a keynote speaker or if you attend one of his multi-day seminars. His successful track record in the business world and his unique approach is a breath of fresh air to companies across America.

Russ, welcome to *Pillars of Success!*

Russ Rogers (Rogers)

I appreciate being here!

Wright

When we hear you speak about getting rid of the rules, it sounds pretty radical. So what do you mean by "getting rid of the rules"?

Rogers

I ordered at the drive-through today and they messed up my order; but I'm sure they have a rule or policy about messing up an order. Thousands of laws are passed each year yet they don't seem to help. Companies are hiring lawyers by the dozen to see how thick they can make their employee handbook but I don't see the return on that investment. It seems obvious to me there are plenty of rules, laws, and policies and it's equally obvious more rules and laws aren't working.

Since more and more rules, policies, and laws don't seem to be the answer, the answer must lie somewhere else—in the heart or attitude of people. If we focus on our culture and our values, we could theoretically do away with all the rules.

I told my son he couldn't play basketball in the house. He was fine with that until a while later when I heard a crash in the house I realized he broke a picture while he was playing baseball in the house. I shared with him that we had just talked about playing basketball in the house and he quickly replied, "You didn't say anything about baseball!" Naturally he was correct, but you would think even a six-year-old could have made the connection. I immediately made a rule; he couldn't play any kind of ball in the house. Twenty minutes later another crash resounds through the house and I notice a dent in the wall made by a Frisbee. I realized at that point I was going to have to inventory the whole house and make rules about each and every object in the house, what he could do and couldn't do with each piece of merchandise he finds.

I took a few moments to restore my sanity and went to my son to chat about the situation. Some people call this lecturing, but I like to tone it down a bit and refer to it as a chat. He was open minded and was quick to share with me I never said he couldn't throw the Frisbee in the house and that playing Frisbee was not really a sport. I knew when I sat down to chat that I could not come up with enough rules to make sure everything was going to be perfect. I knew the only way I could get across to him is to reach his heart. If I could instill in him the value of our property, he would not do anything to destroy it. In a few short minutes I found the words to explain to him the value of the property and he was fine with that. Other than some isolated incidents, we have yet to have an issue with our son destroying our home because he had a heart change.

A businessman who employed over one hundred people called me and shared with me all the problems he was having in his company. He had upset customers, upset employees, and he was spending most of his day playing firefighter—putting out little fires all day every day. I met with him and he showed me his five-hundred-page policy manual which outlined all the rules. He wanted to hire me to teach his five-hundred-page policy manual to his employees. Not only was I *not* going to read his manual, I certainly wasn't going to take six months of my life to do so.

I shared with the man that his employees simply did not care about his company and therefore they didn't care about the customers. I explained that he probably had good people, but they didn't understand their role in the bigger picture enough to care the way the owner of the business cared. I suggested that we work on the employees "hearts and attitudes" and the rest would be fine. Reluctantly he agreed.

We held some education classes to inform employees how their specific job contributed to the whole company. We brought in some customers to share their experiences. We put in some production spiffs for employees, and implemented employee appreciation programs, just to name a few. In less than six months his business was up over 50 percent.

Work on the culture of your organization and you'll soon be able to toss out the rules.

Wright

What sets you apart from other equally talented people? Why are you successful where others are not?

Rogers

Equally talented? Heck, most people are a lot more talented than I am. However, my energy level and my willingness to keep going when others quit will typically put me on top.

Whatever I'm doing, I try to be the hardest working person in the group. I'm the first one up in our home and most of the time the last one to go to bed. Other than the NBA, Andy Griffith, and the Crocodile Hunter, I seldom waste time watching television. I know people who waste so much of their life sitting in front of the television set wondering why they are overweight and broke. If the kids are in bed and you email me at eleven at night, chances are I'll respond immediately.

In any job I've ever had I was the first one to work and usually the hardest working person in the building without question. It's my nature to give 110 percent of everything I do regardless of how tired I am, how inconvenient it may be, or how poorly I feel. People who get a sniffle and call in sick will never be successful. It's not that I want people to go to work sick, but when people do this they are really looking for any excuse they can find to get out of work. The people who trudge forward no matter how they feel and without regard as to whether or not someone is standing over them watching every move, have a much better chance of being successful at whatever they do.

When I'm on an airplane, in a hotel room or waiting on a flight at the airport, I have my laptop out, I'm jotting down ideas, I'm working on a book, I'm reading a book, etc. My colleagues will sleep on the plane, hang out at the bar at the airport, and sit in their hotel room watching television and they wonder why business is so bad. Go figure. Of course, when the NBA finals are on, I'm one of those folks glued to the television.

Wright

What would you say would be the biggest contribution to your professional success?

Rogers

My failures. I would not be as successful as I am today without my failures. I was recently asked, "If you could go back in time and change some of your mistakes, what would you change?" I'm not sure that I would want to change anything—especially the failures. I made some pretty dumb financial decisions that resulted in losing just about everything I had at the time, but I wouldn't dream of not going through that for what I learned and how many opportunities I've had because of what I learned.

I remember giving a speech to a company and I wasn't prepared as I should have been. Admittedly I was ashamed the presentation I made that evening. The audience was pleased but I knew and the meeting planner knew I hadn't been prepared. I refused to accept payment for that event and offered to do another event for them at no charge with a promise I would be better prepared. Was I prepared the next time? You bet I was and I decided that evening I would never go unprepared again. Now I probably do the overkill in preparation but had I not failed miserably that day, I wouldn't have the preparation work ethic I have now.

All my setbacks have made me stronger, wiser, and overall a much better person. Why would I want to be weaker, dumber, and a worse person?

Wright

You mentioned you learned from your failures, so how do you handle those bumps in the road and make something positive out of them?

Rogers

Unless the sky is not blue in your world, those bumps in the road are coming! Since I know they are coming and I know ahead of time that bumps in the road will make me better, I accept that on the front end and it makes the process much easier.

I'm reminded of the time when I was playing ball with friends and my wife threw me out at home plate. When I got to home plate I slipped on a bat, and although I've never had any knee problems in my life, I really messed it up that time. I had to learn new words like "ACL Reconstruction and Meniscus tear." It was painful, the surgery was no fun, and the physical therapy made the dentist look like my best friend. However, I am a runner and I now appreciate running more than ever.

I had friends come to my side to offer help when I didn't even know they knew me that well. At that time in my life I needed to slow down and when it happened, I had no choice than to slow down. It also gave me time to finish a book I was writing. Once again, what was viewed as a huge setback turned out to be one of the best things that ever happened to me. If I had to do it over again, I wouldn't change a thing.

I made a huge mistake once in the company I was running. The mistake cost the company thousands of dollars and I just knew I would soon be fired. The owner of the company talked to me about it and although he was not thrilled at losing thousands of dollars, he said he would not fire me because anyone could make that mistake. He said that mistake will probably make me one of his top executives and additionally, he said he sure didn't want to hire someone else and have them make the same mistake. He was right. That mistake helped me grow and of all the companies he owned, we were at the top and remained at the top. My huge mistake, as always, turned into a huge positive. Again, I already know I have more bumps coming my way and I've already decided that I will be a better person when I go through the process. It's easier to decide now, beforehand, that setbacks are positives rather then when you are in the middle of the fire.

Wright

As you go to train companies across America, what do you want to instill up-and-coming executives about corporate America.

Rogers

Hire me! I'm kidding, but I'm serious about what I would like to say to every up-and-coming superstar: Implement some absolute personal values and stick to them. With all the corporate scandals you hear about, there is someone behind the scandal who had no absolute personal values; they compromised their integrity, and now will be facing a lifetime of shame. All that could have been avoided if every young future corporate superstar would decide by the first day on the job that no matter what—no matter what it could cost, no matter if it cost money, cost a promotion, or even their job—they will never compromise their integrity or the integrity of the company. Think about it—if you have to compromise your integrity to be promoted at a company, why in the world would you want to be a part of that company?

I had an acquaintance who was asked to do something blatantly wrong by his boss. His boss was adamant that he complete the task, and his boss insinuated in his instructions that his job would be in jeopardy if he didn't. I asked my friend what he was going to do and he said he didn't know what to do because he needed the job to feed his family, and pay his mortgage among other things. It was obvious he was really struggling with what to do. However, had he already made the decision to never waiver from integrity, he would not be in this position as he would have already said no to his boss. Going against my pleading, sadly, he went along with his boss's instructions, both of them ended up getting fired, and he had to face his wife and children to explain why he was no longer employed.

Make that decision *before* you begin your first day on the job because it's easier to make that decision before you are in the circumstances of someone offering you a raise if you'll fudge on some numbers in accounting, share a small lie to a customer, or tell just part of the truth rather than all the truth so you can make that sale. Put some absolute values in your life, stick to them no matter what, and never waiver from those absolutes.

Wright

You talk about taking the small steps, what do you mean?

Rogers

I used to work with a comptroller who would always say if you take care of the little things, the big things will take care of themselves.

An example is when I was just out of college and I began running. I called myself a runner even while my running regime was to run three quarters of a mile from our house, fall down in someone's yard, try not to lose consciousness, and walk back with the hopes I would see a friend who would drive me the rest of the way home.

One day Mr. Robert Smith, age sixty-seven, was sitting across from my desk wearing a Peachtree Marathon t-shirt. I could see that Mr. Smith and I were on common ground because both of us were obviously runners. Assuming Mr. Smith was not presently a runner due to his age, we began talking running. I immediately realized that I was the only one present who was not a runner. Mr. Smith was still running five miles every day and ran twenty miles every Saturday. That was all the motivation I needed to really become a runner. I ran three miles the next day and didn't die! I bought some real running shoes and I was able to run a little farther. I acquired some running clothes so that I wouldn't get so hot and I ran farther and farther. I began running earlier in the day when it was cooler and I could go even farther. I learned what to drink and not drink before running and within a few months I could run over ten miles. Was it the motivation? Was it the shoes? What it the clothes? Was it the fluid intake? The answer is "yes"—it's all of them. I did a lot of little things that added up to big things.

On a side note, it was funny because I ran through the same neighborhoods for many years and noticed other people out exercising. For five years I didn't see a single other consistent exerciser. Some people would start walking and others would begin running. I could see they had brand new tennis shoes, a Walkman, and they were set. Most of the time in less than two weeks, I would never see them again. I would go to work and I would normally be the most fit person in the building and people would call me lucky. I got up by five o'clock every morning, ran thirty-five to forty-five miles every week for five years, ate right, and was not overweight, yet I was "lucky." No, I wasn't "lucky"—I took care of the little things and the big things took care of themselves.

The same is true for being successful. Most people are waiting on that one big life-changing event to take place that will catapult them into success and it's not going to happen. I played the trombone in high school and when all my friends were out riding around or sitting around playing video games, I was practicing. When they sat on the couch after school watching television, I was either taking lessons or practicing. When my friends would sleep until noon on Saturday, I would get up early and practice. When it came to tryout for the All-State Band, I became the number one trombone player in the state and most of my friends didn't even get close. Of course, I was told what a "natural" musician I was; but the difference was I worked on the little things for months and months when others were not willing to do so. I found myself at the top and they found themselves at the bottom wondering what happened. Once again, I took care of the little things.

Business people ask me all the time what's the one thing they can do to really make a difference and they are always surprised that the answer is that there's not just *one* thing.

Most organizations want to get better but they usually wait until they are in trouble and then they want that "magic bullet" that makes everything okay. I was called by one of these companies to help them with some problems. I shared with them we need to implement about twenty ideas and over time they would become very successful. The owner wanted to retire and knew he couldn't unless some aspects of the business changed. Therefore, he agreed to support my ideas.

We trained front line people in how to handle customers. We educated people so they could see how they fit into the big picture. We took ideas from employees, who typically have the best ideas, and put them in action. We stopped some expenditures that everyone agreed were a waste of money. We developed a way to hold people accountable for their productivity and devised a method to track their progress. I could go on and on, however, we didn't do one big magical feat that changed the business—we worked on a lot of little things and I'm happy to report that business is doing better than ever and the owner is probably sitting on the beach right now in Maui reading this book.

One reason this is such a key factor is because if you are waiting on that magic bullet, not only will you not find it, but you'll probably not do anything to help your organization in the meantime until you find yourself in trouble and have no other choice. By then, it's usually too late.

Take yourself and your business off autopilot and take care of the little things so the big things will be in place to take care of themselves.

Wright

I understand you use humor a lot. I know you're not a comedian but how does humor help you become successful?

Rogers

I find humor in just about everything. Ironically, the humor I usually share is about the crazy things that happen to me. The same things that happen to me happen to a lot of others and people appreciate knowing someone else has been there with them. Once people understand I am not that much different than they are, I suddenly become more effective in reaching them and adding value in their life.

Here's one example of why you should look beyond your circumstances. I attended a very important business meeting at a fairly nice restaurant with about twenty or so business people in attendance. An *hour and a half* into this forty-five-minute luncheon and seventeen glasses of iced tea later I had to go take a break.

On my way out of the restroom, I did what I always do in that as soon as I turned on the faucet, I started to pull down on the lever to retrieve the paper towels. As a typical guy, my history was not to worry so much about cleanliness. (When our first daughter was born all that changed and I have grown fond of germ-free living.)

This trip to the restroom was no exception in my attempt to avoid germs at all cost by trying to not touch anything once my hands were clean. By turning down the paper towels, once I finished washing my hands, all I had to touch would be paper towels which meant I could use the paper towels to turn off the water. What I failed to notice was that the faucet was broken. As soon as I turned on the faucet and reached for the paper towels, water shot out across the sink and I now had water shooting at me and hitting me in the worse place possible. It's important to note that I was wearing Khakis and now I have this dark circle giving the impression I hadn't made it in time to the restroom.

I was then thinking, "This is not happening!"

I began searching for the hand dryer so I could dry my pants when I realized that I must be in the only restroom in that city without a hand dryer. I thought this would really be funny if it was happening to someone else. Then it hit me. If it would be funny then, it's funny now. Why? Because they know what kind of person I am and when you know the person, little things like this are no big deal. I went back to the meeting, we all laughed, had a good time, and it was truly funny. To this day if I see someone from that meeting, they will start laughing.

Most of the time we get all upset about something but when we look back, those instances were really no big deal. People can relate to being in embarrassing circumstances making me more effective in reaching people.

Wright

What message do you want to get across to the readers in this book?

Rogers

Start right now. Whatever it is you want to do, start right now.

I'm not so naïve as to think most people will start right now, but that's the answer. People are waiting for their ship to come in and it's already here disguised as lots of hard work.

My first speech took me over six months to write. I wrote it, re-wrote it, practiced it, practiced it in front of friends, practiced in Toastmasters, and got lots of feedback all for a forty-five-minute speech on a subject I could speak on with my eyes tied behind my back. When I finished my speech more than one person came up to me and said, "You are just a natural born speaker. I wish I could do that, but I could never get up there and do that. You are very good and I bet it helps being good at it naturally." Quite frankly, I wanted to hit them (okay, not really). But in reality they could have given the same speech as well as I had if they were willing to do what I did to give a great speech.

The same thing is true in any profession. The successful people are willing to put in the hours that others are not willing to do. I remember watching Jerry Rice with the San Francisco 49ers after he had just won the Super Bowl and was getting ready for the Pro Bowl in Hawaii. Here is the best receiver that ever lived and he was the only one in Hawaii practicing while the rest of the NFL players were lounging around the pool talking about how lucky Jerry Rice is. That's exactly what successful people do while the rest of the population says, "Russ, you are just lucky." Ask anyone close to me and they will tell you that I work harder than anyone they know and because I am successful, I'm considered lucky. Go figure.

It took me two years to write my first book. I wrote a little here and a little there and two years later I had a book. I had a friend who said, "I wish I could write a book but I just don't have the time." I shared with him that it took me two years and encouraged him to just get started. Five years later, still no book. Why? He never got started.

Start *right now*, take whatever small steps you need to take, but get started right today.

Wright

You mentioned balancing success with family life. So how do you do that?

Rogers

I make my family a priority. My family is not something that I take care of when I don't have anything else to do. I actually have on my calendar "Family Night" for certain nights of the week. If someone calls and wants me to do so something that night, I will say with all honesty that we have plans.

Every year after the Christmas holidays, I do what every parent does in that I ask the question, "What did you do that was the most fun? What was your favorite thing you received or *gave*? What had the most meaning to you during the holidays?"

One evening our family was gathered around the table and I posed the big question even though I already knew the answer. I knew what my little boy would say because I gave him this cool toy that he loved and had been playing with every day since Christmas.

I knew what my girls would say because my wife had picked out some beautiful dresses to go with their dolls and I'd witnessed them playing with the dresses and their dolls constantly since they opened their gifts.

I already knew the answers but I posed the question anyway.

To my surprise, my son said, "Daddy, the most fun I had was when we played hide and go seek in the dark with you and Granddaddy."

Wow! You could have knocked me over with a feather.

My girls agreed that the most fun they had was when the whole family stayed up late one night eating popcorn and got popcorn all over the bed watching *It's a Wonderful Life*.

Here I'm supposed to be teaching my kids what matters most and *they* were teaching *me*!

I am so busy now I am forced to live by my calendar. I have blocked time to exercise. I literally have time with the family on my calendar. I have "date with daughter" on my calendar.

I knew early on that I would never be seventy years old looking back wishing I had worked more.

If your family matters to you, you'll make them a priority.

Wright

What are some stumbling blocks our readers are facing today that will keep them from being successful?

Rogers

The biggest stumbling block is all in their head. This sounds so simple but it is so true. I've heard this concept my whole life but it wasn't until a few years ago that it really sank in—you really have to believe you can do something before you can do it. Sounds corny, but hang on a minute. Here's an example: if I don't believe I can catch any fish today, I'm probably not going fishing. If I believe I can catch fish, then I'm going to go to the trouble of getting my rod and reel ready, buying some bait, getting the boat out of the garage, and before you know it I'm on the lake catching fish.

If you don't believe you can do something then you won't jump through the hoops it takes to accomplish it. If you don't think you can run five miles you won't even try. If you don't think you deserve a promotion you won't even try to get it. If you don't think you can get that great job, you'll not even apply for the job. If you don't think you can mend that relationship with a coworker, you won't even try.

I have a friend who is probably the most qualified person I know for a certain job. He really wants the job and he really thinks he would truly be great at the job. I've seen other employees of that company so I know my friend could do as well as or better than anyone in the company. However, he doesn't believe they will ever hire him. Since he does not believe they will hire him, he has not even filled out an application. Most likely, if he would fill out the application or send in a resume, they would hire him. I talked to someone at the company and they are interested in him coming to work, yet he thinks they won't hire him so he won't even fill out the application. Every time I chat with him, however, he talks about how much he would love to work for that company. The only thing keeping him from his dream job is believing he can get the job.

I helped a department of a large company with several communication issues. They believed the morale was so low that nothing could be done. I tried a couple of things and I didn't get the immediate fantastic response I was hoping to receive. I was greeted with some "I told you so's." I spent the whole next morning with the executive team attempting to convince them the morale could be improved without burning the place down and starting over. One executive after another came on board during that meeting and by the end of the meeting we had devised a plan that everyone was excited about. No surprise to me, it worked. What's ironic is that the plan the executives and I implemented is the same plan I had in the beginning. The only difference was now the executives believed the plan would work.

Whether it's increasing sales, improving a relationship with a spouse, finding time to spend with your family, getting a promotion, getting on a budget and saving money, or increasing productivity in your company, if you don't think you can do it, you'll not do anything to even get started.

There are other stumbling blocks to success, but the first one you'll have to overcome—the one in your head—must be overcome before you can move on to the next one. If you believe you can do something, you'll go to the trouble it takes to do it. If you don't, you won't.

Wright

Well, what a great conversation, I think I've learned something here today! I really do appreciate all the time you spent with me Russ. I think that our readers will really get a lot out of the comments you have made and I just want to tell you how much I appreciate your taking the time to do it.

Rogers

David, it's my privilege. It's an honor for me to chat with you today and I hope I have helped.

Wright

Today we've been talking with Russ Rogers who is a proven leader in the business world. Russ has devoted himself to helping companies succeed through his communication, his leadership, and his teamwork training. He has spoken to several large companies throughout the nation and he just keeps his people captivated whether you hear him as a keynote speaker or whether you attend one of his seminars.

His track record in the business world is good and his unique approach is a breath of fresh air as you have found out here this afternoon.

Russ, thanks a lot for being with us on *Pillars of Success!*

Rogers

Thank you David!

About The Author

Still married to his high school sweetheart, father of four, and over fifteen years of business experience, Russ Rogers enjoys nothing more than helping individuals, companies, and organizations grow beyond their wildest expectations. Russ is a member of the National Speakers Association, International Speakers Network, and has enjoyed speaking to major companies such as Honda, Asbury, Eastman, DTS, CC Homes, NADA 20 Groups, schools, and many non-profits, just to name several. Whether you are a non-profit organization, church, or major company, Russ can put his experience to work for you. Additionally, he is helping families across America with his newest book, *The 17 Laws of Parenting.*

Russ Rogers

3605 Rockwood Place

Kingsport TN 37664

Phone: 423.782.7001

E-mail: russrogers@chartertn.net

Chapter Thirteen

PAT BENDER

David E. Wright (Wright)

Today we're talking with Pat Bender who is the president of Bayley & Bender, Inc. Prior to co-founding Bayley & Bender Pat worked for IBM Corporation. In her first year with IBM she achieved "Rookie of the Year" by selling 140 percent of quota and went on to claim top performance awards for the next ten years—a rare accomplishment. For four consecutive years Pat was in the top 2 percent in performance at IBM and was honored with four Golden Circle awards. During her final year at IBM Pat earned the distinguished award as the top sales representative in the country. As a manager Pat built and trained a sales force which finished as the top team in the country. She holds a BS degree from the University of Maryland. She is one of the few Certified Professional Behavioral Analysts, Certified Professional Values Analysts, and Certified Attribute Index Analysts in the world. She is a member of the National Speakers Association, the American Society of Training and Development, the Training Officers Conference, Society for Human Resources Management and the Women's Initiative Alexis de Tocqueville Society, United Way of Central Maryland. Pat has touched people's lives from Canada to the South China Sea, from India to the Caribbean. Pat speaks about the behavioral styles and values that affect individuals, organizations, and the federal government. Whether working with steel workers from Baltimore, Maryland, the federal government, or corporate executives from all over North America, England, Finland, Norway, and Portugal, Pat brings awareness, fun, creativity, and insight into her programs. This is probably one of the reasons she is a popular keynote speaker on a number of international cruises, including the former Seabourn Sun, Seabourn Spirit, QE2, Crystal Harmony, Celebrity Horizon, Oceania Regatta, the Silver Sea, and the Sea Dream Yacht Club.

Pat Bender, welcome to *Pillars of Success.*

Pat Bender (Bender)

Thank you, David. It's a pleasure to be here.

Wright

How do you help people in business?

Bender

We help people in business through our AWARENESS IS POWER® process. Everything we do focuses on Awareness Is Power®, raising people's awareness of themselves, and how they effectively work with others. So we offer insights to organizations that are already successful. We take them to a whole other level. We are noted for Leadership Development, Building Highly Effective Teams, and we help develop World Class Sales Teams.

Wright

How do you develop people into World Class Sales Reps?

Bender

In the words of our client, Bruce H. Williams, VP Integrated Technology Services IBM Global Services, "In the Awareness Is Power® World Class Selling seminar, the sales team learned how to put the "heart" back into selling, which is a forgotten art that is critical to building sustainable relationships with customers in a competitive environment. Through this session, our sellers became more aware of their strengths and areas for improvement in sales execution. In addition, the teams learned new strategies for communicating more effectively with customers and inside our company."

Bob (My husband and partner) and I have discovered that World Class Sales Reps have five things in common:

1. **Leave No Stone Unturned.** I learned this from Bob Bender. He said to do everything you can possibly do in an account to generate business.

2. **When they say no, that's when the selling begins.** My boss at IBM, Bill Duffy, taught me when someone tells you no, you are closer to a yes. He always said when you get nine no's the next one is going to be a yes. When someone tells you no, you need to figure out why they are saying no so you can re-strategize.

3. **Always have a reason to come back.** Bob Bender said whenever you talk to people, always have a reason to come back. Send them something. Whenever you make a sales call, at the end of the sales call, set another appointment to keep things moving for follow-up.

4. **Be Yourself.** That was the advice my father always gave me. Whenever I was going for a job interview or going to make a big sales call he would always say, "Pat, just be yourself." And when things didn't seem to work out, I would go back and examine why it didn't work. It was because I forgot the lesson my father taught me: Be Yourself.

5. **Sell with Heart.** My father, who is a natural born musician, taught me to play the accordion. And what I remember most is that he said, "Pat, play with heart." One of the first songs he taught me was, "Love Makes the World Go 'Round." I'd sit there and watch everyone's expression as they listened and watched my father play. He really is great and what makes him so great is he always plays with heart He really feels his music. He was also a life insurance agent, so I grew up in the world of sales. But when I started selling for IBM, that's when something just started to click. I started selling the same way I played "Love Makes the World Go 'Round"—I could "feel" the products—I was selling with heart. And that's another secret to being a top sales person—you've got to have heart.

This is what H-E-A-R-T means to us:

H stands for Happy. I was at University of Maryland Cole Field House the other night talking to Juan and Pam who are student workers. We started talking about being happy. They asked, "What does happy mean to you?"

"Happy to me," I replied, "is when I am in New York City, on Broadway, and boat riding."

Juan said, "It seems like you have this a little out of order. New York is really big and Broadway has the lights and the action, but boat riding? Anyone can go boat riding."

"Not the boat riding I'm talking about," I said. "I like to cruise in our boat from Annapolis to New York City going right past the Statue of Liberty as the sun is setting."

Pam said, "What's the name of your boat?"

"It's called *Let the Good Times Roll!*"

H also stands for Humble. A humble person is kind, thoughtful, gracious, and willing to help—a good person. Humble people are other oriented.

E stands for Energy. When we are happy we will automatically have energy and we want to build our energy. We have energy when we do the things we love to do and have the right resources to do what we want. Your resources come from understanding yourself and that is Awareness.

E also stands for Empathy. Be able to step into someone else's shoes. Bob says empathy is putting yourself in the place of the other person.

A stands for Ask Questions and Listen. Know your products and services so well that you know the right questions to ask. And after you have asked the question pause and listen for at least five seconds without interrupting. Be patient.

A also stands for: Availability. Be available to your customer after you have made the sale. This is service, service, service! Even if service isn't part of your job, your customers will never forget you. This is how you get excellent referrals.

R stands for Read your Customers' Voices and Tones. We teach salespeople how to read voices and tones and to identify the different behavioral styles.

R also stands for Rapport. Build rapport with your customer— sell yourself before you sell your product or service. Establish credibility. If you gain rapport you have gained friendship and credibility. They like you and you like them.

T means be True to Yourself. Have an awareness of yourself. What are your strengths? What are your limitations? What are your blind spots? Awareness also means be fully present and in the moment. And when you are fully present and in the moment, you will have fun!

T also stands for Trust. To build trust it takes faith, it takes openness, and it takes a sensitive part of you and making that available to someone else. That's when you are connecting—your heart with another's heart.

We have developed a process where people can assess these five things and gain insight into their abilities in each of these five areas. We call it the "HEART TEST." What does the Heart Test focus on? What characteristics are assessed in the Heart Test? It measures happiness, humility, energy, empathy, asking and listening, availability after sales, reading tones, building rapport, truthfulness to self, and trust.

Wright

How have you helped companies develop their leaders?

Bender

Once again, we've helped them through this Awareness Is Power® process. We believe that awareness is unlimited. The more aware you are, the more aware you'll become. The way that we help people, we say that leaders or successful people have three things in common:

1. Successful people have the power to see themselves, which means they know themselves inside out and backwards.
2. Successful people have the power to see themselves with others, which means they're able to identify, understand, and (the key) *appreciate* the people that are different than they are.
3. Successful people have the power to win in every single situation because they're able to adapt their behavioral style to what the situation is calling for.

Wright

I love the catch phrase "Awareness Is Power®." How do you define it?

Bender

We have a registered trademark for Awareness Is Power®. Awareness is unlimited. The more aware you are, the more aware you will become. Once you have awareness you have the power to have, to be, to do whatever you want in life. You have the power to communicate with people the way they want to be communicated with. You have the power to be happy. Awareness gives you a tremendous amount of power for whatever you want in life.

Wright

I've read in your materials that you can read someone in less than sixty seconds. I'd love to be able to do that. Can you tell us how you do it?

Bender

Sure. We can read people in sixty seconds or less just by watching them—by the way they walk, by the way they sit, by the way they stand. It's really fun. We can go into a restaurant and just by the way people move their hands we can detect different behavioral styles. We can do this by noticing how a person sits in a chair, and if the person's hand is on his or her chin, we read what behavioral style the person has. We notice people standing on a street corner. If a person is pointing his or her finger at somebody, that's a certain behavioral style. We can also tell by the tone of the voice.

Wright

If I knew this information, would I be able to communicate effectively with others?

Bender

Absolutely. That's the power of awareness because when you understand your behavioral style, you can read someone else in sixty seconds or less. Then what you will do is communicate in their language because people like to be communicated to in *their* language. When I'm communicating with you I'll figure out what your behavioral style is and then I'll talk to you using your style.

Wright

Does this have anything to do with happiness? Can all people find what will make them happy in life if they know these kinds of things?

Bender

Oh, sure. The real key to happiness always starts with yourself. You find out what makes you happy. We have Awareness Is Power® assessment tools which create seventeen different reports. Our most popular version is the Awareness Is Power® Leadership report. It is very powerful. It reveals your individual power traits. When you read this report it's at least 85 to 95 percent accurate.

We'll go into organizations and specialize in team building, world class selling, and leadership development. People might block us out thinking, "Oh, there's nothing you can teach me about team building," or, "I already know all about this." But then when they see their report and they read the first two pages revealing individual power traits, and they realize how accurate it is, they'll say, "How did you learn about me? How do you know this about me?" We'll say, "We bugged your phone; we bugged your office." Of course, they know we are joking.

The first time he ever read his report Bob said, "I felt like someone crawled into my body and read my heart, my soul, and my mind and put it on paper." That's how accurate it is.

The next page on the leadership report reveals your unique talents and all of the strengths and values you bring to an organization. Most people don't really focus on what their talents are. They just take it for granted.

When we do read somebody's report I'll tell him or her, "These are really great."

The reply will usually be, "Well, doesn't everybody have this?"

I'll say, "No. This is what makes you so special."

People don't even realize they have these special talents. When you start doing things that make you happy and you use the talents you have, whether it's in your work or in your personal life, that's what's going to make you happy.

Then we go to a much deeper level. We go into values. Behaviors are how you do what you do. Values are why you do what you do. When you're starting to live your values then you can't miss. Eighty-five percent of the people in today's workforce do not like their jobs. When you can match somebody with the right behavior, the right values in the right job, then that person is going to be happy.

Wright

As you have developed your company and your life, what has been the biggest challenge you've had to overcome?

Bender

The biggest challenge that I have overcome is my husband's health. On June 8, 1995, we found out at three-thirty in the afternoon that he had an aneurysm in his abdominal aorta and it was twelve centimeters. It is normal to operate on a six-centimeter aneurysm. We were on a plane at seven o'clock that night to the Cleveland Clinic and the next day he had emergency surgery. We shut the business down for three months. Within two years and two months he had four major surgeries. In 2003 he had another aneurysm in his thoracic aorta. It was a twelve-hour surgery and we shut the business down for a year.

Bob has had seven miracles and we count our blessings every single day. The biggest challenge was getting him back to health, shutting the business down, and then bringing it back up again. It's been a challenge, but it's been successful because when we shut the business down the first time, after three months the business was just incredible—it was booming. It was totally incredible. God sent people into our lives left and right.

Wright

And his health today?

Bender

His health is good. He has an aneurysm right now, but we live one day at a time. We do our best and say a lot of prayers.

Wright

I'm interested in this matching people to their ideal job. I, too, have read articles stating that 85 to 87 percent of people get up and drive to "hell" every morning because they hate their jobs, which is hard for me to understand. What do you do to match people to their ideal job?

Bender

We have an entire process. Once again, it's our Awareness Is Power® process and this is the "Hiring Winners" option. We'll work with individuals and then we'll also work with organizations. So if we're working with an organization, we'll benchmark the job and then we'll say, "Okay, what does the job require?" We measure it in three different areas. We measure it behaviorally, how the job works, and why the job works, and what capabilities and talents are needed for the job.

Once we do that, then we'll help the organization. We'll put the candidates through an entire assessment of behaviors, values, and competencies. When we work with individuals we have a Career Choices report—*Awareness Is Power® Career Choices*. It's really incredible because at the end it has a job indicator listing the jobs that are best suited for individuals' behavioral styles. We'll be able to say, "You would be perfect as a nurse," or, "You'd be perfect as a lobbyist or talk show host or engineer."

We will then take it one step further and assess their values. They might want to make money or they might want to help people.

People are happy with the process because they end up in the careers that give them their true passion.

Wright

When you consider the difference between attitude and aptitude, what difference does attitude make in people's lives?

Bender

Attitude is everything. If you see the glass half full then you're going to be a much happier person. We believe that attitude is extremely important. Have you ever seen somebody who walks around with a black cloud over his or her head? My neighbor, Jack, has a black cloud over his head. Last October I was walking out to my mailbox and Jack was walking out to his mailbox. I said, "Hey Jack, we lit a candle for you in church yesterday."

He said, "Don't waste your money and don't waste your prayers."

"Jack, how you can say that? You prayed really hard for Bob when he was sick and now we're praying hard for you."

He said, "You know, I kept telling those doctors for three years something was wrong with me and they could never find out what was wrong. Now they've found lupus and I'm never going to get better; I'm only going to get worse." He said they could have done something about it three years ago, but now it's too late. "I'm never going to get better. I'm only going to get worse," he said.

"Jack, you can't think that way." But he just stood there leaning on his cane saying, "I'm never going to get better, I'm only going to get worse."

Well, there was a black cloud over to our right and then it started coming toward us and then the sky just opened up, but I happened to have my "magical" umbrella with me. When I opened it up I said, "Hey, Jack, what do you see?"

"I see a black umbrella for this doomy, gloomy ugly day," he said.

That's the view that some people have of life. It's a negative view or pessimistic view. Then I flipped my umbrella so he could see the inside and said, "Jack, what do you see now?" Inside there are blue skies and clouds. That's the other view that people see. It's an optimistic point of view. You have two choices. You can either look at the black umbrella or you can look at the inside of the umbrella, which has the blue skies and the clouds. When you look at the happy side you're going to be happy. Life always has its challenges. You never know what is around the corner. You could be walking down the street and everything's going great. But it doesn't always go great. It's the way that you look at life.

Wright

We were talking a moment ago about communicating with people and treating them in the way they want to be treated, or communicating with them the way they want to be communicated with. What are some of the different communication styles?

Bender

In certain behavior styles you'll encounter one type of person who is bottom-line, results oriented. This individual wants you to be short, brief, to the point, and stick to business. When talking to these people, be prepared with support materials in a well-organized package. You may encounter certain things that are going to create tension or dissatisfaction. For this particular person don't talk about things that aren't relevant to the issue. Don't leave loopholes or cloudy issues.

There's another type of person whose behavior style is magnetic, enthusiastic, friendly, demonstrative, and political. You want to provide a warm and friendly environment with them. What's going to create tension is being curt, cold, and tight-lipped.

Another person is a patient, predictable, reliable, steady, relaxed, and modest kind of person. You want to begin with a personal comment to break the ice. What's going to create tension for these kinds of people is rushing headlong into business.

Another person is dependent, neat, conservative, a perfectionist, careful, and compliant. You want to prepare your case in advance because what's going to create tension or dissatisfaction for these kinds of people is pushing too hard or being unrealistic with deadlines.

This is a quick snapshot of different behavioral styles and different kinds of people. Birds of a feather flock together. It's really easy to communicate with somebody who is just like you. Only 18 percent of the population has a dominant behavioral style just like mine. True leaders will always adapt their behavioral style. They don't expect others to adapt to their style—they will adapt to others'.

Wright

I'm always interested in mentors, helpers, and teachers—those who have chosen their roles accidentally and those people who have purposely chosen those kinds of vocations. Will you tell me of someone you've met who has taught you as much as you have taught him or her?

Bender

That's really a tough question because when I wake up in the morning, especially when we're doing our seminars, I always say a prayer. I say, "Dear God, please open up my heart, my soul, and my mind and please open up every person's heart, soul, and mind. Please have them teach me what you want me to be taught today."

I think the person who has taught me the most is from way back in my IBM days—George Dailey, an executive vice-president at Maryland Casualty Insurance Company. He said, "Pat, you think too small. You need to think big." When I was in sales I had a quota. He opened my eyes to a whole new world because he always said, "You think too small." From that point on, I started thinking big. I didn't begin to teach him as much as he taught me. I am forever grateful to George.

It seems like people are always teaching me much more than I'm teaching them. There are so many people who have taught me so much and I'm forever thankful.

I have another friend who is just the most creative person I've ever met in my life. She is very kind and very sincere. Her name is Michele Deck and she actually is the co-designer of our courses; over time we have developed them together.

There have been so many people who have taught me so much; but I can't leave out our dear friend and mentor, Judy Suiter. She is an awesome teacher. She has taught me so much about behaviors and values. I am forever grateful to Judy, George, Michele, and so many people who have touched our lives and taught us so much.

I hung on to every word Bill Bonnstetter has ever taught me. Bob and I are forever grateful to Bill for everything he has done for us and for Judy, George, and Michele and for so many other people.

Wright

What, in your opinion, is the way to work with difficult people? Some folks have jobs where they don't have a choice; they must work with difficult people. Can anything that you do make that process easier?

Bender

It goes back to awareness. Awareness is just so powerful. When people understand themselves, they understand what their strengths are. We all have strengths, but too much of anything is not good—too much food, too much drinking, too much candy. It's not good and it's the same with your strengths. If you push your strengths too far they become overextended and then they become a limitation.

So, regarding people who are difficult, deep down in their heart they're good—everybody's a good person. If a person is in the wrong job then we can help him or her recognize that and to find another job. But if the person decides to stay where he or she is sometimes it's like light bulbs going off. They say, "Gosh, I didn't realize I was acting like this." Once people start to understand what their blind spots are they can understand their limitations and then they want to be better people—they want to do a better job. Once they're able to do a better job then they're able to work better with other people.

Wright

I know one of your favorite topics is synchronicity. Would you tell our readers, what synchronicity is and how it has worked in your life?

Bender

I love synchronicity. Synchronicity is when a series of events happen. We just had synchronicity yesterday. We were on a boat trip this past weekend celebrating the Fourth of July holiday. We were in St. Michael's, Maryland, and we were staying at the St. Michael's Harbor Inn and Marina. We were going right across to get fuel at the fuel dock. The name of our boat, as I have already told you, is *Let the Good Times Roll*. Beneath the name is our home dock in Annapolis, Maryland. The person on the fuel dock was talking to my husband

and he said, "You're from Annapolis. Are you going to Annapolis right now?"

"Yes," Bob replied.

"Could I hitch a ride?" He was the son of the owner of St. Michael's Marina fuel dock.

We said, "Sure."

When he boarded our boat he was so happy and so thankful. He said, "I can't thank you enough."

I said, "That was synchronicity." He looked at me like he didn't really know what I was talking about, but that was synchronicity. Synchronicity happens every day, maybe as often as ten times a day. When you keep your eyes open and have awareness you notice it happening constantly.

Wright

Is there a specific person or specific personality type that makes the best leader?

Bender

No. It goes back to awareness. When you understand your behavioral style and you understand other people's behavioral styles, the real key is to appreciate the other people. The best leader is the one who is going to adapt to other people's styles. It's not a certain behavioral style that makes the best leader. It's the leader who adapts to others' styles because a really good leader gets people to do things that the people want to do. If you're adapting and you treat people kindly and nicely, others will follow you—you'll be a leader. Leaders get people to follow. You can't be a leader if you don't have followers. If you're not treating people like they're the most special person in the entire world then it's hard to get people to follow you. A really good way to get people to follow is to connect with your heart. When people see that you're sincere and you truly care about them, they'll follow you anywhere, any place, any day, any time, and any time of the day.

Wright

What have you done in your life that you're the most proud of?

Bender

I am most proud of marrying my husband Bob. I asked Bob to marry me 365 times, at least! I've said that was the hardest sale I ever made in my life and after I did that I could sell anything! It's been a really great marriage and not only a great marriage, but it's been a great business. We started the business together and he's as great a partner as he is a husband—he's a fabulous business partner. I'm so thankful every day for Bob.

Wright

I'm finding it hard to believe that *you* asked *him*.

Bender

I did! His wife died and he was single for about nine years. He said he was never going to get married again. She was hit by a car crossing the street in front of their house. It wasn't in my plans to marry Bob Bender, but he came into my life and the rest is history. We celebrated our twenty-year anniversary a couple weeks ago on June 22.

Wright

Congratulations!

Bender

Thank you; it's been great.

Wright

How can someone who is successful move to the next level—go above and beyond?

Bender

We have an entire process. We have phase one, phase two, and phase three.

Phase one is when we talk about behaviors—how you go about doing the things you do.

In phase two we talk about values—why you do what you do.

In phase three we have this incredible process; it's called *Awareness is Power® Personal Excellence.*

When we present these seminars everything is customized. People have told us emphatically they want more. I still remember when we were doing some work at IBM in Atlanta and we were building a team. We asked, "Okay, what do you want to accomplish?" They wanted a seminar on building trust.

We were working with forty-five executives. I asked the executive who hired us, "You want us to build trust; is that all you want us to do?"

She said, "Yes."

"How do you know that that is an issue?" I asked.

She said, "Let's just put it this way, I did some executive interviews and they said, 'I don't know; let me go look. I left my opinion in the closet.' " She knew she had a trust issue so she brought us in.

We completed phase one and phase two. When we put this process together *she trusted us*. We presented the proposal and explained we were going to break it into three phases: Phase I was Team Building and Phase II was Advanced Team Building. We told them we would need thirty days in between so everyone could process what they learned and experienced. Then we would come back and do Phase III—Personal Excellence.

Well, everybody said, "What are we going to do now?"

She said, "I don't know because Pat and Bob said we're going deeper."

"How much deeper can you go?" they asked.

That's the Personal Excellence course. It goes deeper because it's talking about the seven keys to success: loving relationships, health and energy, inner peace, financial freedom, goals and values, awareness, and personal fulfillment. We talk about your insides. We'll get through to the inside, which is self-concept, self-esteem, and the subconscious.

The subconscious is very powerful; it doesn't know the difference between what's real and what's imagined.

There are fifty-four negative emotions that can weigh you down. The worst one is blame. Once you eliminate blame then the rest of your life will totally take off.

We work at many deep levels of awareness to get people ready to establish their goals. By the time they walk out they have written their personal and professional goals and they have a method for achieving them. We created a goal card and it's sitting right on my desk. I look at my top three goals every day. That's where synchronicity goes right back into it.

When you called and asked me to co author *Pillars of Success* with Alexander Haag and other authors, that was synchronicity; it was a magical moment. It wasn't an accident, it was meant to happen at that moment. I was just thinking about getting my book written and then the call came in. When you send thought and energy out to the universe it comes right back to you. But you have to be careful what you are sending out. When you send out positive you get positive in return. When you send out negative, you get negative in return.

Wright

What is personal excellence and how can someone achieve it?

Bender

Personal excellence is really going deep within yourself and asking, "Okay, where is it that I am in life right now?" We've got seven keys to success. The first one is inner peace. The second one is health and energy. The third one is developing loving relationships. The fourth is financial freedom. The fifth is goals and values. The sixth is awareness, and the seventh is personal fulfillment.

We have assessments that allow us to track progress. We'll ask, "Okay, where are you right now on a scale of one to ten with inner peace?" Once you figure out where you are in these different areas then you know which area you want to start working on. You can then start to figure out what is getting in your way. Is it that you have negative emotions and are constantly expressing negative emotions? If it is, you can find out what you can do to get rid of them so that you can look at the inside of the umbrella—the blue skies and clouds—and achieve your goal so you can have, be, and do whatever you want in life, because you can.

We all have the power to have, be, do whatever we want in life but there are certain things that get in our way. Maybe we say, "I can't do this because I've always been taught I can't accomplish this," or, "I really don't want to do this." Maybe we don't really have the desire. Personal excellence is being the best that you can possibly be in your personal life and your business life.

Wright

Would you give us an example of personal excellence in action?

Bender

Personal excellence in action for me is what I constantly work on. It's eliminating the expression of negative emotions. If I'm talking to somebody and he or she wants to get into a negative conversation it only takes two minutes to get dragged down; it's really easy to get into a negative conversation. I'll say, "I have to go now," or I'll change the subject or say, "I don't want to talk about this—let's talk about something positive." It's too hard to get back up once you're dragged down. It's back to awareness. How am I thinking right now? Am I thinking positively or am I thinking negatively?

Wright

It seems as if you've enjoyed your business a lot with your husband. Tell our readers, what have your clients taught you?

Bender

Our clients have taught us so much. We did some work at Bethlehem Steel Corporation. It was such a powerful moment. It was probably in 1997. We worked with the union workers and they would take the training on their time off. They would work sixteen-hour days. If they started their shift at three thirty in the afternoon they would do a double shift, get off at seven o'clock in the morning, take a shower, come into the career center, and sit down at eight and start taking the course. But it was on their time off so they weren't getting paid to take the training.

This process was over the course of about a month in June of 1997. We were completing our entire Awareness Is Power® process which was the Personal Excellence seminar. I still remember this. It was about ten minutes before the course was over. We asked the question, "What is your major definite purpose?"

A gentleman raised his hand and said, "Bob, you've been focusing on the wrong thing for the past three months." Are there ever times in your life, when terrible things happen? This was the month of June; three things really bad happened for Bob. Number one: his father had just died, and his father was his best friend. Number two: he found out that he had to have his fourth major surgery—the fourth major surgery he'd had within two years. I can't remember what number three was, but that was enough. So this man (whose name is Keith) said, "Bob, you've been focusing on the wrong thing. You keep focusing on your health. Stop focusing on your health because you are going to be okay. Your major definite purpose is you're my role model.

"I shouldn't say this, but I'm going to say it anyway. I've been suicidal several times in my life until I met you. And you have made a major impact in my life. I never wanted to work for anyone—I can't stand working for people, but I'd work for you in a heartbeat. You've literally changed my life. Look at everything you've been through. You've had three major surgeries in less than two years, your father just died, you just found out that you have to have your fourth surgery; but just look at you. You have an incredible sense of humor, you have charisma, you are magnetic, you dress impeccably, and you have incredible wisdom. You're not only my role model, but you're every single person in this room's role model."

Then every single person stood up and said, "Yeah Bob, you're my role model. You're my role model. You're my role model." I captured everything on the flip chart.

I had started the business in 1989 and throughout this process the goal was when it was stable Bob was going to jump over. So I was getting the business stable and it really took off three months after he had that first surgery. Remember I said things really took off?

Keith said, "You've been getting in your own way. This is your major definite purpose."

Bob kept saying, "I can't do this business. After thirty years with IBM I can't do this business."

Keith said, "You are a role model and you have taught us so much."

So I captured this on the board. That was a very powerful moment—to be taught by those we came to teach.

We're constantly learning from our clients. We get so much more. When we finish our seminar we're bouncing off the walls and then we realize, "We are so blessed to be doing this." It's totally life changing. People tell us all the time it's life changing.

We did some more work at Bethlehem Steel Corporation. Nick was a very bottom line, results oriented person. He had a lot of blind spots. He had no idea that he had all these blind spots. On graduation day Nick presented us with gifts on behalf of the entire class. It was just amazing. He said, "I want to take you to lunch and I want you to meet my wife."

We met his wife and she said, "I don't know what you did to my husband. I was ready to get divorced. He's a totally different person now."

This all came from the whole process but it was that powerful Personal Excellence course that really did it. It's the whole process. You can't do Personal Excellence without the process.

To sum it up, we mix the "soft" science of human behavior with the "hard" science of analysis.

Wright

I was going to ask you a final question about what you have taught your clients and I think you just answered that question without me asking it. What a great conversation. I really appreciate all the time you've spent with me here today and it's been enlightening to me. I know that people reading this book will get a lot out of it. Thank you so much, Pat, for the time you've spent.

Bender

Thank you, David.

Wright

Today we've been talking with Pat Bender who is the President of Bayley & Bender. She worked for IBM for many years and won every sales record that they have such as Rookie of the Year and went on to claim top performance where she achieved 140 percent of her quota. She also built a major sales team.

I think this work she and her husband are doing now has some real value to our readers and to everyone they touch.

Pat, thank you so much for being with me today on *Pillars of Success*.

Bender

Thank you David, and thank you so much for inviting us to be part of this book.

About the Author

If you're looking to:
- Develop a sales force that really understands the customer
- Build High Performance Teams
- Define, develop, and retain top talented employees
- Grow leadership talent and bench strength
- Improve communication skills and personal effectiveness
- Benchmark performance and personal output . . .

Look no further than Pat Bender.

As president of Bayley & Bender, a people development firm founded in 1989, Pat and her husband Bob have helped thousands achieve personal and organizational excellence through their unique Awareness Is Power® process.

Using her award-winning sales skills and people savvy, Pat offers keynotes, seminars, executive coaching, and training programs for corporations, associations, and the federal government. Four times a year, seminars are offered to the public on an open enrollment basis. Other programs have highly customized content for specific companies and organizations. For Pat's full credentials, please read the introduction to this chapter! To grow your skills and the skills of the people around you, contact Pat Bender personally.

Patricia C. Bender

Internationally Renowned Behavioral and Values Analyst

Bayley & Bender, Inc.

2024 Powder Mill Road

Silver Spring, Maryland 20903

Phone: 301.439.8317

Fax: 301.434.3317

E-mail: aip@awarenessispower.com

www.awarenessispower.com

(Photography on our book covers by Cheryl: www.photographybycheryl.com)

Chapter Fourteen

CURTIS ZIMMERMAN

David Wright (Wright)

Today we're talking with Curtis Zimmerman, founder of The Character Institute. As a premier novelty entertainer for twenty-five years (mime, juggler, and fire-eater), Curtis has incorporated his extraordinary talents into a highly interactive message specializing in the topics of performance optimization, leadership, goal setting, and the role failure plays in success.

Curtis has presented thousands of workshops and lectures throughout the United States and abroad. He has appeared on every major television network and has been featured on numerous television programs. Curtis worked as an entertainer for more than eight years at Universal Studios–Hollywood, Knott's Berry Farm, and other venues. For two years he was a headliner for Carnival and Regency Cruise Lines.

Curtis was named Universal Studios Entertainer of the Year and was also nominated for National Speaker of the Year by the Association for the Promotion of College Activities (APCA). Most recently he was honored with the prestigious 2005 National Leadership Award for outstanding service from United States Congressman Tom Reynolds.

Curtis is author of *I Believe . . . What do You Believe?* and co-author of *Keys to Success in College and Life.* He is a contributing author to *Leadership's Greatest Hits.*

Both as a speaker and as an author, Curtis Zimmerman has impacted millions of people throughout the nation with his life-changing messages and award-winning programs. Curtis is one of the nation's premier entertainers. He mimes, juggles, eats fire, and mesmerizes his audiences with magic. His secret is that he also uses these skills to be one of the most inspirational speakers you'll ever encounter. His goal is to educate people to be character driven leaders who make ethical decisions, handle conflict creatively and take responsibility for their actions. Curtis will give you the tools and the confidence to *Live Your Life At Performance Level.*

Curtis, welcome to *Pillars of Success.*

Curtis Zimmerman (Zimmerman)

Thank you. I'm excited about being here.

Wright

I see on your Web site that you've been selected as an NCAA speaker. How's that going now?

Zimmerman

It's great. I love to speak with college students around the nation, particularly with student athletes. It is crucial to remind them that it's important to strengthen their athletic skills and abilities without forgetting to focus on their academic abilities in the classroom. They are *student* athletes and "student" comes first for a reason.

Wright

If I get a bunch of the alumni together, do you think you can do anything for the University of Tennessee's football team this year?

Zimmerman

Well, I can't perform miracles but I would do my best.

Wright

Getting down to the seriousness of this topic, one of your keynote programs is titled "The Magic of Leadership." What is "The Magic of Leadership"?

Zimmerman

Well, I titled my keynote "The Magic of Leadership" primarily because of my background in entertainment and magic. Over the years of performing I had the opportunity to work with some Master Magicians. I would always try to learn from them. For example, when I was performing at Universal Studios in Hollywood, I would share a break room with all the different acts. I would offer to share some of my learned skills in mime and juggling in exchange for a new magic trick or fire-eating technique. It was not necessarily the most talented or most "famous" people who shared the best trade secrets but it was the "real people" as I like to call them.

As I made my transition from entertainment to inspirational education and started developing my message, those early experiences came back to me. The real leaders in my life were those who were not afraid to share their "magic," knowledge, skills, and secrets—giving away to others. What I encourage people to do is share the magic you have—everything you possess. It only does you, your community, and the company you work for any good if you actively give it away. That's really where the "magic" part of it comes in.

The topic is the magic of *leadership* and leadership has so many different definitions, shapes, and forms. I always say that if you're taller than my knee, you're a leader to someone. I think all people have the ability to step up into a leadership role but they lack the courage, or the sense of community or concept of giving back to actually take the chance to step out onto that limb.

Wright

Why is leadership training so important in today's corporate culture?

Zimmerman

Great question—this subject is making headlines in the newspapers on a weekly basis. The reason why leadership training is so important is because corporations are realizing that they need to get back to the fundamentals of what leaders do. Some corporations question whether the young, fired-up bucks who will be running their company in future years have the leadership style that the corporation desires. They are now more than ever valuing and spending their resources on leadership training, knowing that the future of their company may depend on instilling character, ethics, and decision-making skills on their young, entry-level workforce who haven't learned these skills elsewhere.

Wright

What is the difference between formal and informal leadership?

Zimmerman

Formal leadership is what we typically think of as a leader has. It may be a title, a position, or a level of status earned or imposed upon an individual. Title, position, or rank doesn't always make a great leader. I believe the *informal* leadership skills create the greatest leaders. For example, we all have a "circle of influence" which would include the twenty to thirty people we interact with on a weekly basis. This circle of influence may include a child, someone in your department or someone in your neighborhood or in your family who looks up to you. You're being an example, as if those who look up to you are watching you all the time. Remember the golden rule? That's informal leadership.

Wright

What are some practical tips to be a better leader that I could perhaps incorporate in my daily life?

Zimmerman

Practical tips for leadership, in my opinion, boil down to two basic tasks. One is define your belief system and the second one is to "be real." The reason why I say these are practical tips is because so often we are advised to follow "the ten strategies to becoming a leader" or "the thirty seconds you spend every day to be a leader," etc. My problem with most of this advice is that these are conceptual not tangible tasks to implement. I believe in doing the obvious. By evaluating and determining what you truly believe, you can rely on your belief system to make moral, ethical, and value-based decisions.

The second practical tip I mentioned is what I call "being real." In my book, *I Believe . . . What do You Believe?* I wrote that, "I believe honesty is not only the best policy, it cures insomnia." "Be real," then you never have to look back or re-think what you said and wonder if you've covered yourself because of something you said earlier. Honesty, morals, ethics, and values are what I equate with being a great leader.

Wright

So, for example, I've just graduated from college and I'm in the workforce for the first time; how do I spot a leader?

Zimmerman

Look within your circle of influence, find the "real people" whom you respect, who aren't multitasking you, who look at you when you talk and give their undivided attention, and who fully engage in life. Spot the individual who seems to have a strong belief system and is not afraid to share his or her secrets of success like the magicians I met along my path as a performer who were able to "give it away."

Wright

You mentioned mentoring. How does mentoring play a role in leadership?

Zimmerman

Mentoring is something you have to be actively engaged in looking for. I don't care if you're the CEO of a company or it's your first day on the job, everyone needs mentors. We're always growing and learning, changing, and becoming and we need someone who has already been down that path to help us get there. I think mentoring is one of the critical elements needed to become a true leader.

Wright

As you have traveled the country speaking to corporate, college, and military audiences, what are some of the changes or trends you have seen regarding leadership over the last several years?

Zimmerman

Particularly with corporations, in the past I would do a presentation with the goal of getting folks fired up—motivating them for a couple of hours and making them feel great about themselves and the company they work for. But then five or six weeks later, it was as if the experience had never happened.

Now, one of the trends I see is that corporate leaders want me to come in for the initial meeting to get everyone fired up but then they want to have some kind of instrument to keep people on target—to remind them of what happened in the previous session and to really keep their questions, their concerns, and their leadership growth on an ongoing track. Rather than having someone come out for a one-time session, they want to set up something that will have a lasting effect and is somehow quantifiable. I think that's right on target. I love to say that when I visit a company, the corporation's bottom line benefits. I feel even better, however, if I can enrich individual lives, indirectly enriching their families and the community in which they serve. This is something that won't happen as easily in a one-time shot.

Wright

How do our beliefs influence and affect our leadership style?

Zimmerman

We accumulate our beliefs throughout our lifetime from different experiences and different things people have told us. I want people to take time, in whatever season they are in life, to go back over their belief system and search for the origin of their viewpoints. Are the attitudes empowering or limiting? If you have a limiting belief and you got it from a seventh grade schoolteacher fifteen, twenty, or thirty years ago, you may want to reanalyze that script and rewrite it into an empowering belief.

We bring our viewpoints to work, to our relationships, and to ourselves every day. Our beliefs are what guide us to make every one of our decisions. If you ever want to envision yourself as a leader, you have to know what you believe in.

Wright

What do you think the difference is between responsibility and accountability? Most people define those terms as meaning the same thing, right?

Zimmerman

Yes, but I think that responsibility and accountability are two different things. The only way you can truly be what I call "response-able" is by knowing what is expected and being able to respond in the way you choose. So often people base decisions and actions on what I call "old scripts." Scripts are the things that have happened in the past, which include those belief systems I just mentioned. If I am the person I am today based on different things from my past, then I'm going to react to you and your questions, or a given situation, based on old scripts. If you truly want to be response-able—able to respond in the way you choose to respond—you have to look at these circumstances with brand new eyes every time and be accountable for a response.

During my presentations I love to play Simon Says and in about six minutes I can get fifty to as many as five thousand people out. The reason is because people just react—they don't stop and think before they act. They are not being response-able. Responsibility is accepting what is to be done and accountability is doing it.

Wright

In conclusion I would be interested in what you think a "real person" is. In other words, what does it mean to be a "real person"?

Zimmerman

I often say that "being real" is another definition for what I call a real leader. Being real is very simple and yet it's one of the hardest things to do. It means you look at every situation with new eyes, you're an honest person, and you base your actions and your decisions on morals, ethics, and values.

A real person is also not afraid to share something I call his or her "real-sumé." In the beginning of this program you shared my resumé: mime, juggler, Universal Studios, television commercials, speaker around the nation, author—that's a resumé and that's a good thing to have. But I'd much rather have people share something I call their "real-sumés" which includes all the personal things that make them a person—things that would never be included in a job resumé. "Real people" are not afraid to share who they truly are, what they truly believe in, and they're not afraid to act upon those beliefs.

As I said, being real is one of the easiest yet most difficult things to do because it means you're not putting on any masks and you're not trying to become something else in the moment according to the group you're with. I know you've probably heard the axiom, "When in Rome do as the Romans do." I love to say, "When in Rome do as *you* would do." I don't care what circumstance you're in, I don't care what table you're sitting at—be it with your five-year-old child or with executives from companies across the world—who you are as a person shouldn't change based on that environment. You may use a different fork but what comes out of your mouth during that dinner should be the same based on your morals, ethics, and values.

Wright

What an interesting conversation. I really appreciate your taking all this time with me, Curtis, to answer all these questions. I know I've learned a lot and I'm positive our readers will.

Zimmerman

Thank you. It was my privilege to be part of this project and I look forward to speaking with you again, hopefully sometime in the future.

Wright

Today we've been talking with Curtis Zimmerman, a native of Los Angeles, who is currently residing in Cincinnati, Ohio, with his wife and three children. Curtis Zimmerman is one of the nation's premier entertainers. He mimes, juggles, eats fire, and mesmerizes his audiences with magic. His secret is that he also uses these skills to be one of the most inspirational speakers you'll ever encounter. Curtis will give you the tools and the confidence to truly *live your life at performance level*. This means doing what it takes to reach your ultimate potential in every aspect of life. By understanding how everyday reactions and perspectives build the world you create for yourself, you can take charge and be more confident of the life you design and deserve!

Curtis, thank you so much for being with us on *Pillars of Success*.

About the Author

The REAL-SUMÉ: Curtis Zimmerman was born in Torrance, California—his first of many hospital visits. At age sixteen he was diagnosed with a rare disorder called Sprue or Celiac Disease. Because the disease was commonly misdiagnosed, Curtis suffered for years with anemia, seizures, and multiple stints in the hospital—often staying days and weeks on end with no explanation for his illness. He was raised in subsidized housing on welfare and food stamps by a mother who dearly loved him and his four siblings. She also loved her six different husbands and not one of Curtis' brothers or sisters had the same father or same last name. Unfortunately, as a young child, Curtis was exposed to many harsh realities. Alcoholism, suicide attempts, drug addiction, and abuse were common under his roof. His mother liked to move frequently, therefore Curtis attended approximately six different elementary schools, some of which he'd leave halfway through a school year because his family was on the move again—an early summer vacation! Sounds like any young boys dream, however, Curtis has dyslexia and needed school more than most young boys learning to read and write. The purpose of this real-sumé is not to engender sympathy for Curtis or be impressed by the fact that he overcame his disadvantages and his suffering, but to understand that he is where he is today because he was blessed with some "real people" in his life. Individuals saw the gifts he had and wanted to help him find those gifts, develop them, and use them. He met performers who taught him, doctors who really cared and teachers who took the effort to make a difference in his life. His resumé is a tribute to the leaders and mentors in his life and this chapter is dedicated to them.

Curtis Zimmerman

Founder, The Character Institute

Phone: 513.229.3626

E-mail: curtis@curtiszimmerman.com

www.curtiszimmerman.com or www.thecharacterinstitute.com

Chapter Fifteen

HENRY GOUDREAU

David Wright (Wright)

Today we're talking with Henry Goudreau. Born and raised in the construction business, Henry's father was a successful contractor with an education in accounting. Henry spent his early years watching over his father's shoulders learning by observing.

Henry's education is in civil engineering and business. He has worked as a project manager/project engineer for contractors on every conceivable type of construction from residential homes to nuclear power plant construction, nationally and internationally, before starting his own business.

He is the author of several self-study manuals for contractors, the book *How to Market & Sell Your Construction Services Like Magic!* and writes for numerous trade magazines and newsletters each month.

For the past twelve years he has been presenting his forward thinking methods and techniques on managing successful construction companies and has helped numerous contractors achieve enormous successes with their companies through his exclusive "Golden Hard Hat Program."

Henry, welcome to *Pillars of Success*.

Goudreau

Thank you.

Wright

Tell me, how did you get started as a business coach, author, and speaker?

Goudreau

I guess you might say I fell into it. At the young age of forty-three I had the opportunity to go into what I thought would be an early retirement—walk away from my business and try to do some other things. I quickly realized that I needed something more challenging to do—something more rewarding. I thought about it and realized that one of the things I've always attributed to my success and the people who worked around me was going to seminars and workshops and continuing the education process.

When I thought about that I realized how many times I had been in the audience and thought I could present the information better—I understood it better, and I could probably do a better job at presenting it. So as I sat there wondering what I wanted to do with my life, I decided I would take that route and get the opportunity to teach others.

That's exactly what I did. I took a year to two and a half years traveling around with some of the best speakers and coaches, taking a look at their services, what they did, and how they presented everything. I thought it would be very rewarding and it has been *extremely* rewarding.

For the past twelve years I've been very active in the industry. I've spoken at the National Association of Homebuilders, Associated General Contractors, and many other national associations. I've written numerous articles for trade magazines as well as a training manual for the National Association of Homebuilders, and I wrote my own book *"How to Market and Sell Your Construction Services Like Magic!"*

I think I'm helping a lot of contractors by making them understand exactly how their business works and how it falls within their market place and within their own organization.

Wright

Let me understand this correctly—you've actually owned your own business prior to what you are doing now, so how did you draw from that experience?

Goudreau

When I first started, my dad was a very smart numbers man. He understood the numbers and the accounting of the business and I used to learn a lot by watching him. I loved my father so much I always said the last thing I'd ever do is work for him because we were too much the same type of person and we'd always butt heads. I had decided early on in my life that I wanted to own my own business.

When I got out of high school I went into education to prepare myself in the construction industry. When I graduated college I acquired experience by working with the other contractors. That was very rewarding because I was at a point where I could see what they were doing and I realized that they were making mistakes. They weren't managing their business, they weren't controlling the spending, and they hadn't systemized everything that was going on. I could sit there and say, "Wow! If he would do just one or two things he could improve the operation a lot." I actually drew from watching other people and being involved with them.

Then, in my late twenties, when I had the opportunity to start my own business, I drew on that experience to make my business as successful as I possibly could. I always kept asking myself this one important question: "Is there a better way to do this?" What I found, particularly in the construction industry, was that a lot of the people who have come up as business owners have come up through the trades or through the technical aspect of the business such as estimators or engineers. They lacked management skills but they had great dreams—they wanted to be successful and they wanted to grow and have a great business. Because of their lack of management skills, however, they were caught up with a lot of the inefficiencies that they created for themselves in their own business. Instead of building a business and working *on* that business, they ended up working *in* the business—the day-to-day stuff consumed them and the business didn't seem to progress any further than that. It was the same thing every day in-and-out; it never changed. They failed to realize that the real money in any business is made in the management of that business.

Wright

What do you think are the biggest obstacles you find business owners face?

Goudreau

We've done a lot of studies and we've worked with a lot of contractors and typically what I ask contractors is, "Would you build a project without a set of plans?" Their answer is that they wouldn't—they couldn't even begin to do it. Yet, just about every single one of them is trying to build a business without some type of business plan, or a strategic plan. I'm finding that a lot of the contractors today, with all their dreams of success, are running out there, slapping the name of a business on the side of their truck but not taking the time to sit down to think and plan their business—where is my business going to be in one year, three, five, ten years or even twenty years from now? What are the steps that I have to take to get from here to there? What accomplishments do I have to achieve? Even when I've achieved the goal I've set for my business (and I call that "the end result"), what's it going to look like? What's the vision? A lot of them are so excited to get into business they don't take time to plan it, set goals, implement the correct actions or steps to make it happen, or to build a vision.

Without the plan it is almost impossible to achieve or control the desired end result. For example, when expenses are incurred without the necessary revenue benefits, profits decrease. Time is spent trying to get the business back on track. Time is a nonrecurring entity, once time is gone, it is gone; you can never get it back. When the human resources are unproductive because of a lack of understanding, training, communication, leadership, or whatever, then profits suffer. When profit suffers, performance suffers. When performance suffers goals are pushed back. When goals aren't met time is wasted, money is consumed, and profits are lost. It is a never-ending cycle for some business owners—one minute you're up, the next minute you're down.

When marketing and selling produces poor sales or accounts receivable fails to collect cash, then the entire cycle starts over again.

One of the biggest obstacles facing the majority of business owners is the lack of good management skills and knowledge. This is especially true in the construction industry. Practically every contractor came up through either the trades or technical end of the business. They know how to bang the nails, pour the concrete, or tie the wire but they haven't had any training or education on managing the business. Whether a company is a new startup, a mom-and-pop operation, a small or big company, this common thread prevails—a business owner must manage that company's resources. The ability to do so is where the success really comes from. It doesn't come from working longer hours, or from taking on more work than you can do, or even from taking work for smaller margins just to get the work.

Here's a simple story that reinforces my point: When you fly on a commercial airline a lot of "unseen" things happen in order to make that flight happen. Someone drafts up a flight plan that states when the plane will leave, how many people are on board, what the weight factor will be, how much fuel is required, what the weather will be, and so forth. The pilot picks up that plan, verifies it, and then goes to the plane. On the plane they check the systems and criteria, make certain everything is working properly, and the flight leaves. Even with all of this planning, external forces are still attempting to push that flight off its intended course. Now the beauty of having that flight plan is this: With it and all of its information and facts, that pilot can quickly and easily determine what action is necessary to get that flight back on course. He can even determine what action has to be taken to reach its final destination without any delays. Without the plan, he would be lost and without the proper information needed to make the right decision as to what action is necessary. This is how the vast majority of business owners are sabotaging their own dreams of success with their business—they don't have an all inclusive plan and goal for their business and when they get off course they have nothing to draw from to get it back on course or even to understand it is even off course.

I have a saying, "Contractors don't fail for a lack of good construction skills; they fail for a lack of good business skills!" The truth is successful businesses are managed by utilizing known, proven, and tested successful processes, procedures, techniques, and having a business mindset. When you learn and implement them into your business you are actually "optimizing" your business for success.

Wright

Can't they just go out and buy a book, listen to motivational tapes, or attend night school to learn how to manage their businesses?

Goudreau

Well, what I find is the motivational tapes give them a lot of inspiration but they don't give them the nitty-gritty—the small steps they have to follow. One of my biggest selling e-books is, *"How to Calculate Your Mark-Up."* I sell more of this e-book than anything else. What this is telling me is that they don't even know how to mark up their work properly! In this e-book I take them through the whole process of developing a markup, such as: How much profit do you want to make? What are your costs going to be? What do you think your sales are going to be? Therefore we have to mark it up this number to achieve that bottom performance. But they have no idea how do that. They know how to wire the job, they know how to put the lumber or steel together but they don't know how to make the numbers work. That's usually their biggest obstacle. They're finding a lot of books to read and a lot of seminars to attend but the information they're acquiring isn't fulfilling that real-life need.

I've had so many of them come to me and say, "I've been to so many different seminars. I've listened to so many experts but you're the first person who has said, 'Let's put these numbers together. Do you see how they fall into place? This is what you need to do in order to make that happen.'" That's obviously what's lacking as far as the information that's out there right now.

Wright

Since all businesses are different, how do you deal with that?

Goudreau

That is one of the biggest excuses I hear from contractors. As a matter of fact, if you walk into one of my seminars I have a big banner that says, "But Henry, My Business is Different!" The truth is it's really not. I don't care if you're a custom homebuilder, or a framer, or a utility person, there are still very basic business fundamentals that have to be understood and incorporated into your business in order to make it successful.

This is part of what I call "optimizing your business mindset." Now that you're thinking more like a business manager and you're not sitting out there running on sheer guesswork saying, "I think the job is worth this much. I think I'm going to make this much money." We've actually sat down, we've pulled the numbers together, and we know how much work we should have on the books at any given time. This is the information that is needed to make the money. It's not the banging of the nails—it's the management of the people who are banging the nails, the numbers, the materials, and the vendors. This is the real skill that contractors are lacking—it's just that one small skill. It's amazing to see that once they learn it what a huge differ-ence it makes in their business. The difference is like day and night. All of a sudden they have greater control, and are making more money with better customers. But the truth is, because they have taken a positive action step in improving themselves and their busi-ness, each one is now a powerful positive magnet attracting the positive results they desire.

Wright

What are the advantages of having a business coach rather than a consultant?

Goudreau

I think there's a huge difference between the two. If you hired a consultant—say you hired me as a consultant (but I don't do consult-ing work)—I'd come out, I'd spend some time, I'd charge you for that work. I'd look at your business; I'd find what's wrong. I would then write a beautiful report and give it to you; you'll pay me but you won't understand what's in the report. The result is no positive action—no positive results.

I learned that very early on in my career when I first started speaking. Contractors would come up to me and ask to hire me as a consultant to help their businesses. I had a deep desire within me to help them. I would really work on their problems and I'd put together this great idea—this strategy—to correct them and put it in this fabu-lous report and I'd hand it to them. I found it would actually sit on their desk and collect dust. The reason for that was simply because they didn't understand how to make it work. They didn't understand the mechanics or components of how the solution to their problem(s) came together.

So I thought about that and decided I wasn't going to take people's money if I can't help improve their lives. I came up with the idea of being a business coach. Now, what I do is provide all the information and I help contractors implement and master it for themselves and work with them showing them how to do it. I help them learn how to make it work, implement it into their business, and with me by their side, we can make that business work. All they have to do is do the work. This follows along the lines of that old saying, "Give a man a fish, you feed him for the day, teach him how to catch the fish and you feed him for a lifetime."

However there's a key word here and it is "implementation." It's one thing to have all of the knowledge but if you don't understand how to implement it properly into what you're trying to achieve, you're not going achieve success. That's where a business coach comes into play. The coach is the one who helps you identify problems; correct them, implement the solutions, modify it, and change it—whatever you've got to do to help you bring that into your business to do what you want it to do.

That's the difference between a coach and a consultant. I think everyone should have a business coach because the coach is the one who will help you make this work. The coach is going to show you what you need to do to make it work and that's a key piece of information; actually that's the all-important "missing link." You'll never get that from a consultant—you'll get a report, nothing more. Most people don't have the time, they don't understand it, and they're not going to sit down and put the work into it. But if I give you the information and I sit by your side and help you do it—actually walk you through it step-by-step—you've got a better chance at being successful with it.

Wright

Henry, your USP states, "I turn contractors who dream of owning a successful business, into business managers who make a business successful!" What is a "USP" and how does it work?

Goudreau

Your USP is your "Unique Selling Proposition"—that one thing you put on the table that your customer or client cannot get from anyone else. It's what separates you from all your competitors making you and your business the logical or only choice.

If you take a look at my USP statement, I turn contractors who dream of owning a successful business into business managers who make their business successful. That pretty much states exactly what I do. A lot of people have dreams. Why do we start a business to begin with? There are only two reasons: One of them is to be successful—to have money. The other one is freedom of lifestyle. But you have to manage that business. As I said earlier, you have to understand the fundamental equation—you've got to take this business entity and put it on a track that's going to take it to achieving the success we want somewhere out in the future and to achieve all these necessary steps and goals to do that. So that's what I do.

A lot of people go into business dreaming of being successful but what they don't understand is they have to become a business manager, they must have a plan with a strategic focus based on a desired end result. I teach them how to be that business manager with that strategic focus.

Wright

Why would you want to turn a business owner into a business manager?

Goudreau

The answer to that is very simple: Anyone can own a business but it takes the manager to make that business successful. He's the one who has to make all the key decisions setting the business on the right course. He's very much like a captain on a ship. The captain decides where the ship is going, when it's going to leave, and when it will arrive at port. He works out the navigation, he decides how much fuel is needed, how long the trip will take, and he takes into consideration the weather. He's managing that ship—he's understanding everything that's going on with that ship.

A business manager does the same type of thing. Just because you own the business and you hire people and you pay them a week's salary, doesn't mean it's going to run in the right direction, that it's going to have enough of the right fuel, or whatever else is necessary. So managing the business, understanding that someone has got to be the captain, someone's got to determine the course and exactly what is needed to properly fuel and execute the business, that is what we're talking about.

The one person who understands his or her business better than anyone else is the owner of that business. The reason for that is simple. The owner is the one who had the initial dream or vision of accomplishing something by going into business. The owner is the one who determines the course necessary to achieve the desired goals, and is the one who can take that business and systemize it. He or she is the one who can develop the strategic plan to work. The owner knows what he or she wants to achieve with the business—no one else can do that; but the owner has to understand the principles necessary to accomplish it. That's where I come into the picture. I show owners and tell them, "This is how we do it, and these are the steps you have to take. Now let's take your dream and turn it into a reality by building these steps."

There is an old story about how circus elephants are trained. A huge iron pin is driven deep into the ground and a big chain is attached to it. That chain is then attached to the elephant's ankle. Now the chain is short and doesn't allow the elephant to go where it wants to go. Over time, the elephant gives up and accepts his fate. It is then and only then that the trainer removes the chain and the pin and replaces it with a small stake and some rope. The elephant never goes anywhere because he has already given up trying. He doesn't realize that he could easily break free of the rope and small stake and roam wherever he wants.

Many business owners suffer from the same problem. They've accepted their mediocre performance in business very much like the elephant accepted the chain as his fate. Because they won't expand their horizons by learning the right skills they stay shackled to their business. With the right attitude and commitment, I can show business owners how they can profoundly improve their business.

Wright

You talk about vision and goals, how are they different?

Goudreau

There's really a big difference in the two. What I teach my people is the goals are the things we want to achieve. We're going to have a number of goals. We start today to build this business and we want to achieve very specific volume or profit or success with it in ten or twenty years. We're going to have all these steps and each one of them will be goals we're going to have to think out. We're going to have to determine what steps we need to take and what accomplishments have to be made before we make them. These are our goals.

The one single most important thing is what is the end result? What is the vision? Can you see what your business is going to be like in ten or twenty years from now? Can you determine what it's going to feel like to be successful? You really need to have that vision and you need to have a passion to achieve that vision. Otherwise you're going to have a very difficult time making all those steps/goals come into play.

If I remember correctly, when asked why he won so many battles, Napoleon Bonaparte replied simply, "I am focused on my objective, therefore my obstacles must give way."

If you don't have a vision and you don't understand the goals necessary to make that vision a reality you instead become focused on your obstacles, therefore your objectives become clouded or disappear. That's what happens with a lot of people. They want to be successful, they go out and start a business, but they fail to do the planning—they fail to determine the steps/goals they have to accomplish, they don't develop their vision and end result—what they want to achieve and how it's going to be achieved. They don't have the passion for it. So without the plan they get caught up in the day-to-day obstacles and they lose complete focus on what they're trying to achieve with their business.

Wright

Let's talk about the two reasons why people would want to own their own business. What are those two reasons?

Goudreau

Why would anyone want to own his or her own business? There are only two reasons. I call them: Financial freedom and freedom of lifestyle.

To some people financial freedom is very important to them. To others freedom of lifestyle is most important, however maybe they need some financial freedom to live their lifestyle. There really are no other reasons to own a business.

In order to achieve both of those things, you have to understand that there is an economic equation—you have to plan out that route and you have to put that entity—your business—on the right track to achieve all the corporate successes that you have to have reached first so that you get to a point where then you start achieving your personal goals and successes. We have business goals and successes and we have personal goals and successes. We need to get them in the right order and we need to get them on the right track and that's the only way to achieve the two things we're all looking for: financial freedom and freedom of lifestyle.

Wright

You talk a lot about balance or as you call it "equilibrium." Will you explain what you mean by that?

Goudreau

I've learned a lot about balance, or equilibrium, from the many years I have been in business for myself and from something even deeper than that. I've been involved in the martial arts since I've been a young kid. I think I started when I was nine years old. One of the things they teach is balance; they call it the "yin and the yang." You must have balance in your life—in everything. When you take a look at a lot of these businesses it's quite evident that there's something out of balance. The imbalance could be in the financial end of the business, or the productive operation end of the business; it could also be in the administrative or the marketing.

What we try to do with these businesses is to bring them into equilibrium so that every element is in balance and working properly. There's a synergy that happens when we get things into balance.

When we take a look at construction companies, there are basically four separate departments/divisions. One of them is finance administration—how we handle the business end—the office, the clerical and accounting. Another division is the operation end of the business—how we handle the production that is taking place out in the field making sure the job gets built as scheduled and as budgeted. Then there is the marketing of services—how we get out to the right customers who are willing to pay us the right price so that we can build the job that they're going to be happy with. How are we going to get the leads and find all these people? The last element that makes the construction unique from other business is estimating and engineering—how we sit down and calculate the cost of the job and set up the budget and schedule for the job.

All the above divisions/departments have to be in balance. You've got to know what it is you're trying to achieve with the business, how much work you need to have on hand, how much backlog work in process to be done, how much work do you have to go out and find and bid in order to achieve the sales you want, and what type of manpower you need to do this type of work. We bring all these questions into balance by measuring them and bringing them into equilibrium and we then we can have a very efficient organization. Everyone understands their job, everyone understands the goals they have to achieve, we've got the right amount of management or manpower in place, and they've got the necessary tools to achieve them.

When you go into most businesses you will find something out of balance. Often contractors will come to me and say, "I've got all the sales in the world but I've got no cash flow." What's out of balance? Obviously they're selling their work too cheaply or they're not collecting their accounts receivable. We can go in there and find that, show them not only how to correct it but how to systemize it to optimum performance. Once they get that in balance and once they understand what they need to do to correct the problem or problems, things begin to come into balance and the operation starts to move forward efficiently, productively and most important, profitably.

Wright

I'm learning a lot here today. I wish I had talked to you a few years ago. How many times do you hear that?

Goudreau

I hear it quite a lot. It's absolutely amazing to have contractors who are CPAs, and who have master's in business degrees come to me and say, "Henry, when I started my own business I didn't put a lot of forward thinking up front into it and I got caught up in the chaos. You've helped me get back on line." After having been there and done it myself I can tell you it's very easy to get caught up in the day-to-day stuff and lose track of the big picture. That's where a business coach really does come in handy and gets you back on track and gets you to refocus again.

Wright

What makes what you do so advantageous for your client and rewarding for you?

Goudreau

I think it's basically helping people. I had one contractor come to me who was an architect by education. He said, "Henry, I need help." I asked him how I could help him and he said, "I do $4 million in sales and I'm $1.6 million in the hole." Most people would have put a gun to the side of their head and ended their misery but he looked at me and he said, "This business is my passion. This is the one thing I've always dreamed of having and being successful at. I'm not going to walk away from it. I'm not going to walk away from the people who I owe money to. Can you help me turn this business around?

I took a look at his business and told him we could do it as long as he wasn't afraid to do the work. He did it. When you think about it, it was a $3.2 million turnaround on sales of $4 million—an awful lot to accomplish. It took him about eighteen months to do it and it totally changed his entire life. Now he's profitable every single month and his sales are pushing $20 million a year. Without working with me, expanding his business mindset, learning and implementing the necessary business processes I gave him, he wouldn't be enjoying the success he is having today.

That's rewarding to me—I've actually helped someone.

I had another contractor out of Texas—a roofing contractor. He told me he had owned his business for ten years and had only been profitable during his first year. He had mortgaged his house to the hilt and didn't know what to do other than walk away from it; but he didn't want to.

I took a look at his business and told him what he needed to do to be successful. Within seven months of implementing a strategic plan that we had laid out for his business together, he not only had his first profitable year but he paid all of his debt and had money left over. That's rewarding.

Those are the types of people I enjoy working with because they understand there are no "magic pills," there is no quick fix; it's going to take some work and some implementation. If they are given the right knowledge, the right ideas, and the right strategies, and I work with them and they go out and do it, I actually take joy in their achievements. It feels good inside and that's why I like doing it.

The construction business has been very good to me and this is my way of paying something back—seeing people achieve what they initially wanted to achieve when they first started their business; but when they started their business they didn't understand or have the tools they needed to do it. Once they have these things, they can achieve success. It's such a rewarding feeling to see the change that comes to people when all of a sudden this frustrating business—this "animal" that's been out of control—has come under their control, they've gotten on the right track, and are achieving success. They always say to me, "Wow! I can now see the light at the end of the tunnel; I'm coming out of the tunnel. This is great! I know I can achieve this now." And they're absolutely right—now they can. Before that they couldn't because they didn't have the right tools or knowledge. That's very rewarding.

Wright

Today we've been talking with Henry Goudreau. He's the author of several self-study manuals for contractors, the book, *How to Market & Sell Your Construction Services Like Magic!* and he writes for numerous trade magazines and newsletters each month. Today he's been talking about what makes a business a good business and what makes a manager a good manager. I'm one who's going to listen to him and I believe readers will enjoy these principles he has talked about.

Henry, thank you so much for being with us today on *Pillars of Success.*

Goudreau

It's been a wonderful opportunity to sit here and talk and share with you some of the principles or pillars I've found that can actually take people to success. Hopefully it will help others and if it does that, it's very rewarding.

About The Author

Born and raised in the construction business, Henry's father was a successful contractor with an education in accounting. Henry spent his early years watching over his father's shoulders learning by observing.

Henry's education is in Civil Engineering and Business. He has worked as a Project Manager/Project Engineer for contractors on every conceivable type of construction from residential homes to nuclear power plant construction, nationally and internationally before starting his own business.

He is the author of several self-study manuals for contractors, the book *"How to Market & Sell Your Construction Services Like Magic"* and writes for over twelve construction trade magazines and newsletters each month.

For the last eight years he has been presenting his forward thinking methods and techniques on managing successful construction companies and has helped numerous contractors achieve enormous successes with their companies through his exclusive "Golden Hardhat Program."

Henry A. Goudreau, CSL

HG & Associates, Inc.

389 Interstate Blvd.

Sarasota, FL 34240

Phone: 941.377.1254

www.hgassociates.com